Guide to Christian Perfection

By Charles Fitch

TEACH Services, Inc.
P U B L I S H I N G
www.TEACHServices.com

Copyright © 1997, 2005, 2013 TEACH Services, Inc.
ISBN-13: 978-1-4796-0056-4 (Paperback)
ISBN-13: 978-1-4796-0057-1 (ePub)
ISBN-13: 978-1-4796-0058-8 (Kindle/Mobi)

Library of Congress Control Number: 2012953398

Published by
TEACH Services, Inc.
P U B L I S H I N G
www.TEACHServices.com

Contents

Charles Fitch

Charles Fitch was perhaps the most loved of the great Adventist preachers of the early 1840's—a period when many people of all denominations expected Christ to come in 1844 at the close of the 2300-year prophecy of Daniel 8:14. Fitch, a former Presbyterian minister, believed wholeheartedly that Jesus was coming soon. He saw the necessity of a personal preparation for the soon coming of Christ, and magnified the power of Christ to give victory over sin. With Apollos Hale, he developed the "1843 Chart," which was used by most Adventist preachers to show the many Bible prophecies that converged to the 1843-1844 period.

Because of the rejection of the message of Christ's soon return by the large denominational churches, Fitch saw that they were part of spiritual "Babylon," and in Cleveland, Ohio, gave his stirring sermon, "Come Out of Her, My People." Thus, Fitch was the leading figure in preaching the Second Angel's message.

Fitch worked untiringly and unselfishly to prepare a people for Christ's coming. Just eight days before October 22, 1844, (the end of the 2300-year prophecy when Christ was expected to return), he died of pneumonia after baptizing three groups of people in the chilly Lake Erie waters.

Later Ellen G. White, an Adventist who received the gift of prophecy, had a vision of the future in which she was transported to heaven. She wrote: "Here we saw the tree of life and the throne of God…. We all went under the tree and sat down to look at the glory of the place, when Brethren Fitch and Stockman, who had preached the gospel of the kingdom, and whom God had laid in the grave to save them, came up to us and asked us what we had passed through while they were sleeping. We tried to call up our greatest trials, but they looked so small compared with the far more exceeding and eternal weight of glory that surrounded us that we could not speak them out, and we all cried out, 'Alleluia, heaven is cheap enough!' and we touched our glorious harps and made heaven's arches ring." Ellen G. White, *Early Writings*, p. 17.

Views of Sanctification

by Charles Fitch,
Pastor of the Free Presbyterian Church, Newark, NJ.
Guide to Christian Perfection, Vol. 1, No. 8, Feb., 1840.

PREFACE

The Lord Jesus Christ, **"Whom having not seen, I love; in Whom, though now I see Him not, yet believing, I rejoice with joy unspeakable and full of glory"** (1 Peter 1:8), has of late made good to me, vastly unworthy as I am, His own assurance, **"he that loveth Me shall be loved of My Father, and I will love him, and will manifest Myself to him"** (John 14:21). I feel it would be base in me not to acknowledge, that through the amazing condescension of my Redeemer, He has made me to enjoy rich manifestations of His love. I speak of it to His praise. He has taught me to **"be careful for nothing; but in everything by prayer and supplication with thanksgiving let my requests be made known unto God. And the peace of God, which passeth all understanding, shall keep my heart and mind through Christ Jesus"** (Philippians 4:6, 7).

"Out of the abundance of my heart, my mouth has spoken" (Matthew 12:34), and I have given those who attend on my ministry to understand, that it is my belief that God has **"created in me a clean heart, and renewed a right spirit within me"** (Psalms 51:10), that He has made me to know something of the blessedness of **"the pure in heart"** (Matthew 5:8). Some have thought that I was bringing **"strange things to their ears"** (Acts 17:20), and such a report went abroad.

At a late meeting of the Presbytery, the brethren, with perfect propriety, and with the utmost kindness, desired of me that I would tell them **"what this new doctrine is"** (Mark 1:27). I gave them a brief statement of my feelings and views, and answered as well as I was able several inquiries. The Presbytery, then, with perfect propriety, in my apprehension, appointed a Committee to confer with me further on the subject. Of all this, I fully approve. Soon after, I received a note from one of the committee, in which, in a kind and Christian-like manner, he proposed the following questions, and requested an answer.

1. Do you believe that the Bible teaches men are perfect in holiness in this life? (I ask no more than yes or no.)

2. What cases or characters were without sin in Bible history, except Christ? (merely name them.)

3. Of all among the martyrs, whose memoirs have come down to us, how many do you find perfect?

4. In modern times, have not the best of men evidently been sinful more or less, and have they not thought themselves to be so?

5. In the circle of your acquaintance, have those who claim perfection, generally turned out as well as those who feared always?

6. Are those around you who claim this more meek and heavenly than others?

7. Do not perfection people very frequently run into some palpable inconsistencies?

8. Do you avow the belief, that you are generally without sin, in thought, desire, word, deed, or defect?

9. And have you made up your mind, publicly to teach, and defend the position, that there are men among us who are without sin?

I have taken this way to lay myself fully open to my brethren and to the world, because I believe it to be in all respects the easiest and the best; and do greatly rejoice in the opportunity afforded me, to testify to others of **"the riches of the glory of this mystery which is Christ in me, the hope of glory"** (Colossians 1:27). I wish, by the grace of God, to be a living **"epistle known and read of all men"** (2 Corinthians 3:2).

It is my prayer, that God will enable others, as He has me, to say, **"Behold, God is my salvation; I will trust, and not be afraid: for the LORD JEHOVAH is my strength and my song; He also is become my salvation"** (Isaiah 12:2), and thus may they **"with joy draw water out of the wells of salvation. And say, Praise the LORD"** (Isaiah 12:3-4). And may **"the redeemed of the LORD return, and come with singing unto Zion; and everlasting joy be upon their head: and may they obtain gladness and joy; and sorrow and mourning flee away"** (Isaiah 51:11). Then shall **"the joy of the LORD be our strength"** (Nehemiah 8:10).

CHARLES FITCH

Views of Sanctification

by Charles Fitch,
Pastor of the Free Presbyterian Church, Newark, N.J.
Guide to Christian Perfection, Vol.1, No. 8, Feb., 1840.
Newark, Nov. 25, 1839.

Dear Brother,

In compliance with your request and my promise, I will now endeavor, in the fear of God, and under a sense of my accountableness to Him, to give you my views in full, respecting the points embraced in the questions which you proposed to me. I hope you will not consider it in any sense improper that I give you my views at large on the whole subject, instead of a mere categorical answer to your interrogations. I prefer the course I here take, because I wish to present you with a view of the subject somewhat at large, as it lies before my own mind.

Besides, I consider the subject too great, and the interests pending too important to be disposed of in this summary way. I have no desire to conceal or evade any thing, concerning which you or the Presbytery may wish to know of my views.

My design is, as far as in me lies, to be full and explicit. But I fear that I might suffer much, through the misapprehension of others, respecting my own impressions of truth, if I were not to do something more than you propose in your communication.

Allow me, therefore, to open my whole heart to you as a Christian brother should, and having done so, I will most cheerfully and gladly leave the event with Him on whom I have learned to "**cast all my cares**" (1 Peter 5:7), and whose glory is the only object for which I wish to live.

On His guidance, who has said, "**I will instruct thee and teach thee in the way which thou shalt go: I will instruct thee with Mine** eye" (Psalms 32:8); and "**Who of God is made unto me wisdom , as well as righteousness, and sanctification, and redemption**" (1 Corinthians 1:30); and Who has said, "**If any man lack wisdom, let him ask of God, that giveth to all men liberally, and upbraideth not; and it shall be given him**" (James 1:5). I now cast myself while I write. I shall give you such views of truth, and only such, as I feel most willing to meet in the great and dreadful day of account. I shall give them, as far as possible, in Scripture language, that it may be seen on what I rest my faith, and whether I do, or do not, pervert the Word of God.

Permit me, then, to commence by saying that I find myself in my natural state, a transgressor of God's most holy and righteous law; so guilty as to deserve to be "**punished with everlasting destruction from the presence of the Lord, and from the glory of His power**" (2 Thessalonians 1:9).

I also find myself totally unable to make the least atonement for one of all my ten thousand sins, or to find for one of them the least excuse or palliation. In myself, I stand, and must forever stand before the universe, a hopeless reprobate, irrecoverably bound over to the damnation of hell. But I learn in the gospel, that the Lord Jesus Christ, by His atoning sacrifice, has rendered full satisfaction to the justice of God for my sins, and thus opened a way whereby the punishment of my sins may be escaped, provided I have that "**holiness, without which no man can see the Lord**" (Hebrews 12:14).

The all-absorbing question with me, then, so far as my own eternal interests are concerned, is this: How shall I become obedient to that high command of the most high God, "**Be ye holy for I am holy!**" (1 Peter 1:16, quoting Leviticus 11:44). I have, I *can* have, I *ought to have* no expectation of dwelling where God dwells—of being an object of His love forever, and a sharer of the eternal blessedness which He only can give, unless I have a character fully assimilated to His—unless I love with a full and undivided heart, what He loves, and hate what He hates, and *all* that He hates, with a hatred, full, entire, uniform, perpetual, like His own. There must not be in me an approach to any thought or feeling which is not in perfect, full-hearted and joyous agreement, with everything that God is, and with everything that God does. This must be my character, or I *will* never see God's face in peace.

But how shall I come to possess such a character? Every feeling of my heart, in my natural state, is entire opposition to God—there is in me carnal mind, which is enmity against Him. How shall this hatred be made to give place to adoring, enraptured love? There are in me by nature all the elements of hell. Kindled by the touch of God's deserved wrath, they will burn in an "**unquenchable fire**" (Matthew 3:12).

How shall I have a nature fit for heaven? I acknowledge my full obligation to cease hating God instantaneously, and to love Him at once and forever with a full and undivided heart. But "**I know that in me (that is, in my flesh,) dwelleth no good thing: for to will is present with me; but how to perform that which is good I find not. For the good that I would I do not: but the evil which I would not, that I do. I find then a law, that, when I would do good, evil is present with me. For I delight in the law of God after the inward man: but I see another law in my members, warring against the law of my mind, and bringing me into captivity to the law of sin which is in my members. O wretched man that I am! who shall deliver me from the body of this death?**" (Romans 7:18-24).

This is my case. Christ has died for my sins. The government of God is ready to set me free—but who shall save me from "**an evil heart of unbelief, in departing from the living God?**" (Hebrews 3:12). With such a heart, influenced by the temptations of the devil, and the allurements of a sinful world, I am just as sure (left to myself) to sin eternally, as Satan is, and must take up my abode with him forever.

What I need, then, what the exigencies of my fallen nature cry out after, with an exceedingly loud and bitter cry, is a Saviour from sin. It avails me nothing that Christ has atoned for my sins, if I am then cast on my own resources. Holy beings fell before the wiles of that subtle tempter, who "**like a roaring lion, seeks to devour me**" (1 Peter 5:8), and my evil heart will surely make me a willing prey. I am eternally damned unless I can find a Saviour from sin.

I shall never save myself from sin. My spiritual foes stand ready to devour me, and my own evil heart will thrust me into the lion's mouth—into the wide open jaws of hell. Help! Help! Oh, help! is the cry that comes up from my inmost soul. Is there, in the universe of God, any way to save a poor, lost sinner from his own love of sin? Any way to cleanse his polluted heart, and fill it with holiness—pure, perfect, perpetual holiness; without which such an one never can be received to heaven? With this inquiry, my dear brother, I approach the Bible. Has God revealed any such thing as a way of salvation from sin? If such a salvation can anywhere be found, it must be in the Bible; and if I cannot find it in the Bible, then every ray of light goes out from the horizon of my soul, and the eternal night of despair shuts in upon me.

I am indeed told that I may be saved from sin at death; but that is the hope of the Universalist. I may be told that the Universalist has never been born again, and that he who has been born again will surely be saved from sin when he leaves the world; but I know of nothing on which I can safely rest the belief, that death is to be regarded as the means or the time of sanctification. I believe that "**as the tree falleth, so it lieth**" (Ecclesiastes 11:3), that "**there is neither work, nor device, nor knowledge, nor wisdom, in the grave, whither we go**" (Ecclesiastes 9:10); and that if a man leaves the world in his sins, he remains a sinner forever. I believe that this is my only probation, that I must here be saved *from* sin, or never see God's face in peace.

I believe, therefore, that my everlasting interests are pending on the question, whether God has made provision to save me from sin, before I leave this world. To prevent all misconception, I will here say, that I am very far from believing that the regenerate man with the remains of sin, is in the same condition with the Universalist who has never been renewed; but that neither has any reason to believe that death will make any change in his character. *If there is no salvation from sin before death, I expect to be lost.* Here, then, to make the whole subject plain as possible, in the light in which it is apprehended by my own mind, I will make three inquiries.

I.   Has God, in the economy of His grace, made provision to save His people from their sins?

II. If such provision has been made, can Christians avail themselves of it in this life?

III. In what way may the provisions of God's grace become available, to save His people from their sins?

I. Has God, in the economy of His grace, made provision to save His people from their sins?

I find it said to Joseph, by the angel, in relation to the promised Messiah (Matthew 1:21): "**Thou shalt call His name JESUS (that is, Saviour): for He shall save His people from their sins.**" For this very purpose, then, He is my Saviour, to save me from my sins; and this is just the Saviour that I need.

When John the Baptist pointed out Christ, He said, "**Behold the Lamb of God, which taketh away the sin of the world**" (John 1:29). This is what I need, a Saviour to take away my sins. We read also in the Epistle to the Ephesians, that His people were "**chosen in Him from before the foundation of the world, that they should be holy and without blame before Him in love**" (Ephesians 1:4). That He "**loved** the church, and gave Himself for it; that He might sanctify and cleanse it with the washing of water by the Word, that He might present it to Himself a glorious church, not having spot, or wrinkle, or any such thing; but that it should be holy and without blemish" (Ephesians 5:25-27).

In the Epistle to Titus, we read that "**the great God and our Saviour Jesus Christ gave Himself for us, that He might redeem us from all iniquity, and purify unto Himself a peculiar people, zealous of good works**" (Titus 2:14). In the Epistle to the Hebrews, we find Christ presented as the Mediator of the New Covenant, which is this (quoted from Jeremiah 31:33, found in Hebrews 10:16-17): "**I will put My laws into their heart, and in their minds will I write them; and I will be to them a God, and they shall be to Me a people, and their sins and their iniquities will I remember no more.**"

In the third chapter of the first Epistle of John we find it thus written: "**Whosoever committeth sin transgresseth also the law: for sin is the transgression of the law. And ye know that He was manifested to take away our sins**" (1 John 3:4-5), that is, to take away our transgressions of the law, and leave us in a state of obedience. "**And in Him is no sin. Whosoever abideth in Him sinneth not: whosoever sinneth hath not seen Him, neither known Him**" (1 John 3:5-6).

Now, my dear brother, I believe that Christ came "**to save His people from their sins**" (Matthew 1:21); to make them "**holy and without blame before Him in love**" (Ephesians 1:4); to present them "**to Himself a glorious church, not having spot, or wrinkle, or any such thing; but holy and without blemish**" (Ephesians 5:27); to "**redeem us from all iniquity, and purify unto Himself a peculiar people, zealous of good works**" (Titus 2:14); to write His "**law in our hearts**" (Hebrews 10:16); and to "**take away our sins**" (1 John 3:5), that we might abide "**in Him and sin not**" (1 John 3:6).

This, therefore, I believe to be the salvation of the gospel—that Christ came, according to the words of the angel to Daniel, *"to finish the transgression, and to make an end of sins,"* as well as to **make reconciliation for iniquity, and to bring in everlasting righteousness"** (Daniel 9:24), on the ground of which, we might have deliverance from the punishment which sin deserves. I do find then, most clearly and satisfactorily to my own mind that God, in the economy of His grace, has made provision to **"save His people from their sins"** (Matthew 1:21).

I hail this salvation, therefore, as a salvation exactly adapted to my necessities as a fallen being, and while I utterly despair of ever saving myself from sin, I hail the Lord Jesus Christ as a Saviour, manifested to take away my sins, to write His law in my heart, to redeem me from all iniquity, to make me holy and without blame before Him in love, to sanctify and cleanse me with the washing of water by the Word, that He may present me to Himself, not having spot or wrinkle or any such thing, but holy and without blemish.

I have found, therefore, the Saviour and the salvation I need, plainly revealed to me in God's Word; and on the Saviour I cast my soul, my being for time and eternity; in myself a hopeless, helpless sinner, but trusting in a Saviour in Whom **"dwelleth all the fullness of the Godhead"** (Colossians 2:9), and who has made me **"complete in Him"** (Colossians 2:10), so that I may expect, through His salvation, to **"stand perfect and complete in all the will of God"** (Colossians 4:12). This is my hope of everlasting life, that Christ Jesus my Redeemer will save me from my sins: and in comparison with this hope, the whole material universe is to me of less value than **"the small dust of the balance"** (Isaiah 40:15). Take away this hope from me, and you blot out the light of my soul, and leave me in the blackness of darkness forever.

I believe, then, that full provision is made in the gospel to save God's people from their sins.

II. I am now to inquire whether Christians can avail themselves of this provision of the grace of God so as to be saved from sin in this life?

In the first chapter of Luke, I find that Zacharias, being filled with the Holy Ghost, prophesied, saying, "**Blessed be the Lord God of Israel; for He hath visited and redeemed His people, and hath raised up an horn of salvation for us in the house of His servant David; as He spake by the mouth of His holy prophets, which have been since the world began: that we should be saved from our enemies, and from the hand of all that hate us; to perform the mercy promised unto our fathers, and to remember His holy covenant;** *the oath which He sware unto our father Abraham, that He would grant unto us, that we being delivered out of the hand of our enemies might serve Him without fear, in holiness and righteousness before Him,* ALL THE DAYS OF OUR LIFE" (Luke 1:68-75).

Now I believe, that he who serves God "**without fear,** *in holiness and righteousness before Him, all the days of his life*" (Luke 1:75), is saved from sin, *all the days of his life.* I believe that God "**sware to Abraham, our father, that He would grant unto us, that we being delivered from the hand of our enemies might serve Him without fear, in holiness and righteousness** *before Him,* **all the days of our life**" (Luke 1:73-75), and that He hath raised up an horn of salvation for us, to perform this mercy promised to our fathers, to remember this holy covenant, this oath which He swore. I believe all this on the testimony of a man filled with the Holy Ghost.

Since, therefore, I believe that God's oath can be relied on, especially since Christ came on purpose to fulfill that oath, and since that oath does pledge the grant of walking be fore God in holiness and righteousness all the days of our life, I am bound to believe it. I dare not sin against God by believing that God is not ready to be faithful to

His oath; an oath, too, which Christ came on purpose to fulfill. I read that "**he that believeth not God hath made Him to be a liar**" (1 John 5:10). I must not make God a liar by saying He is not true to His oath.

Again, when the disciples of Christ said, "**Lord teach us to pray**" (Luke 11:1), He directed them to pray, "**Thy will be done in earth, as it is in heaven**" (Matthew 6:10). If God's will is done in heaven by sinless obedience, we are taught to pray for the same thing on earth; and I cannot believe that Christ has taught us to pray for a thing which He is unwilling to grant.

Again, we are taught to pray that "**the very God of peace will sanctify us wholly; and preserve our whole spirit and soul and body blameless unto the coming of Christ**" (1 Thessalonians 5:23); and we are assured that "**He that hath called us is faithful, and will do it**" (1 Thessalonians 5:24). Again, "**If we confess our sins, He is faithful and just to forgive us our sins, and to cleanse us from all unrighteousness**" (1 John 1:9). *As faithful, I suppose, in the one case as in the other. I know of no reason for waiting for forgiveness or cleansing till death.*

In the further proof of the position that Christians may avail themselves of God's grace, so as to be saved from sin in this life, I will here speak directly in reply to your question, "**Who, besides Christ, mentioned in Bible history, were free from sin?**" I quote the words of one, who exclaimed in view of his bondage to the law of sin and death, "**O wretched man that I am! who shall deliver me?**" (Romans 7:24). In reply to his own interrogation, he answers, "**I thank God through Jesus Christ our Lord**" (Romans 7:25). He says, moreover, "**There is therefore now no condemnation to them which are in Christ Jesus, who walk not after the flesh, but after the Spirit. For the law of the Spirit of life in Christ Jesus hath made me free from the law of sin and death. For what the law could not do, in that it was weak through the flesh, God sending His own Son in the**

18

likeness of sinful flesh, and for sin, condemned sin in the flesh: that the righteousness of the law might be fulfilled in us, who walk not after the flesh, but after the Spirit" (Romans 8:1-4).

Paul, therefore, found out a way, whereby to be free from the law of sin and death, and to have the righteousness of the law fulfilled in him. This could be nothing less than loving God with all the heart and his neighbor as himself; for he who does less than this is a transgressor. The law could not do this, in consequence of the weakness of the flesh, but God did it through Christ—fulfilled in Him the righteousness of the law, and thus made him free from that law of sin, under which he had before groaned in condemnation. He was now free from condemnation, but how those can be free from condemnation who are continually sinning against God, it is impossible for me to understand. He hath found, that to those *in Christ Jesus* there was no condemnation, and John tells us that those who abide in Christ sin not.

Paul also says, in another place, that "**he that is dead is freed from sin**" (Romans 6:7). Now if we be dead with Christ, we believe we shall also live with Him. If we die unto sin after the likeness of Christ's death, we shall walk in newness of life, after the likeness of His resurrection. Christ, being raised from the dead, dieth no more, death hath no more dominion over Him—neither if we be dead to sin, will sin any more have dominion over us. Hence, the injunction of the Apostle, "**Likewise *ye* also** (that is, as well as I) **reckon yourselves to be dead *indeed* unto sin, but alive unto God through Christ**" (Romans 6:11). Reckon yourselves to be dead unto sin by trusting in Christ to keep you thus alive.

It may perhaps be said, that a person may reckon himself dead to sin, who has once repented, though he now continues to sin every day. But if I should find a man every day intoxicated, I should not regard him as dead to that sin, whatever he might say respecting past repentance—and the same is true of every other sin in thought, word, or deed. No man is dead to sin who commits sin—and as Christ who died once, dies no more, so he who is dead to sin, sins no more. If he falls into sin, he is no longer dead to sin. Such were the sentiments of Paul, and as I cannot accuse him of the gross inconsistency of preaching what he did not practice—I must believe that he was dead to sin and alive unto God, and that being free from condemnation in Christ Jesus, he did so abide in Him that he sinned not.

Again, we hear this Apostle saying in another place, "**I am crucified with Christ: nevertheless I live; yet not I, but Christ liveth in me: and the life which I now live in the flesh I live by the faith of the Son of God, who loved me, and gave Himself for me. I do not frustrate the grace of God: for if righteousness come by the law, then Christ is dead in vain**" (Galatians 2:20-21). I cannot conceive that a man could use such language as this, who was living day by day in sin. If a man is crucified with Christ, he must be dead to sin, and such an one the Apostle has already told us is "**freed from sin**" (Romans 6:7). No man can say, I am fully persuaded, "**I live; yet not I, but Christ liveth in me**" (Galatians 2:20), who knows himself to be living in sin. Nor can one who lives in sin say, "**The life which I now live in the flesh I live by the faith of the Son of God, who loved me, and gave Himself for me**" (Galatians 2:20). Paul said, "**I do not frustrate the grace of God**" (Galatians 2:21). I do not expect to work out a righteousness by my own unaided efforts to obey the law. I rely on the faithfulness of Christ who loves me, to keep me.

Peter also learned, that "**the divine power of Jesus our Lord had given unto us all things that pertain unto life and godliness, through the knowledge of Him that hath called us to glory and virtue: whereby are given unto us exceeding great and precious promises: that by these we might be partakers of the divine nature, having escaped the corruption that is in the world through lust**" (2 Peter 1:3-4).

I cannot doubt that Peter had experienced in his own heart what he wrote, and I believe, therefore, that in being made partaker of the divine nature, through the "**exceeding great and precious promises**" of God, and "**having escaped the corruption that is in the world through lust**" (2 Peter 1:3-4), he did so "**abide in Christ that he sinned not**" (1 John 3:6). John also declared in his first Epistle unto those to whom he wrote, "**that which he had heard, which he had seen with his eyes, which he had looked upon, and his hands had handled of the Word of life**" (1 John 1:1). He wrote that, therefore, which was to him a matter of experience. He had seen and felt in himself "**that in God was light, and in Him was no darkness at all**" (1 John 1:5), and that when any man walks in the light—in fellowship with God,—"**the blood of Jesus Christ His Son cleansed him from all sin**" (1 John 1:7).

John had also seen and felt that "**If we confess our sins, He is faithful and just to forgive us our sins, and to cleanse us from all unrighteousness**" (1 John 1:9). John had also learned from his own experience that Christ "**was manifested to take away our sins**" (1 John 3:5)—He had "**seen with his eyes, and handled**" (John 1:1) this truth.

He had also learned that "**whosoever abideth in him sinneth not**" (1 John 3:6)—that "**whosoever is born of God doth not commit sin; that his seed remaineth in him:**" and that while this is true "**he cannot sin, because he is born of God**" (1 John 3:9). I cannot doubt that John was a man who reduced his own principles to practice, especially as he wrote only what he had heard and seen, and handled of the Word of Life, and therefore that he did so abide in Christ, that he sinned not.

Thus, dear brother, I have shown you conclusively, to my own mind, at least, that in the economy of God's grace there are provisions available to enable the Christian to walk before God "**in holiness and righteousness all the days of his life**" (Luke 1:75), and so to abide in Christ that he "**sinneth not**" (1 John 3:6). In so doing, I have given you my views in full, respecting the attainableness of holiness in this life, and the question whether any have actually attained it.

III. I am to consider how the provisions of the grace of God become available to the Christian's sanctification?

Our Saviour's prayer was, "**Sanctify them through thy truth: thy word is truth**" (John 17:17). By what truth is the Christian sanctified?

1. Not by any precepts of the Bible, through his own unaided efforts to obey them. So long as any man attempts to become sanctified by this means, he will surely "**find a law in his members, warring against the law of his mind, and bringing him into captivity to the law of sin**" (Romans 7:23); and will constantly find occasion to say, "**O wretched man that I am! who shall deliver me?**" (Romans 7:24).

2. The Christian *may be sanctified* through the promises of God's truth. "**Having therefore these promises, dearly beloved, let us cleanse ourselves from all filthiness of the flesh and spirit, perfecting holiness in the fear of God**" (2 Corinthians 7:1), "**according as His divine power hath given unto us all things that pertain to life and godliness, through the knowledge of Him that hath called us to glory and virtue: whereby are given unto us exceeding great and precious promises: that by these ye might be partakers of the divine nature, having escaped the corruption that is in the world through lust**" (2 Peter 1:3-4).

3. Let me be fully understood, then, that no man is ever sanctified, who relies on his own efforts to obey the law.

Such an one frustrates the grace of God. He would indeed be holy, if he loved God with all his heart, and his neighbor as himself; but this he surely will never do, by any unaided efforts of his own. It must be done by the grace of God, and he most surely "**frustrates that grace who does not live the life he now lives in the flesh by the faith of the Son of God**" (Galatians 2:20).

We are, therefore, to cleanse ourselves from all filthiness of the flesh and spirit, by the promises of God. These contain the truth, through which we may be sanctified, according to our Saviour's prayer.

Two inquiries here arise:

1. What has God promised?
2. How shall we gain the fulfillment of the promises?

First,

1. What has God promised?

I remember that it is said, "**Now, to Abraham and his seed were the promises made**" and that "**if ye be Christ's, then are ye Abraham's seed, and heirs according to the promise**" (Galatians 3:29, 16). When I find a promise in the Bible adapted to the necessities of my case, as I am one of Abraham's seed if I am Christ's, I am one of those to whom that promise was made, and I am an heir to all the good which God, in that promise, has pledged Himself to bestow. With this assurance I look to the promises, and inquire, with eager interest, what has God my Redeemer promised to give me? Here I may look through the whole Bible, for to Abraham and his seed were the promises made, and I am one of them, because I believe in Christ.

"**And the LORD thy God shall circumcise thine heart, and the heart of thy seed, to love the LORD thy God with all thine heart, and with all thy soul, that thou mayest live**" (Deuteronomy 30:6). It is very plain that he who did thus love God, would not sin. The reason why this and other exceeding great and precious promises have not been fulfilled to all God's professing people in every age, will appear, when I shall come to show how we may gain the fulfillment of the promises.

"**Then will I sprinkle clean water upon you, and ye shall be clean: from *all* your filthiness, and from *all* your idols, will I cleanse you. A new heart also will I give you, and a new spirit will I put within you: and I will take away the stony heart out of your flesh, and I will give you an heart of flesh. And I will put My spirit within you, and cause you to walk in My statutes, and ye shall keep My judgments, and do them. I will also save you from all your uncleannesses**" (Ezekiel 36:25-27, 29). If it should be said that those promises were made to the Jews, I reply, "**to Abraham and his seed were the promises made**" (Galatians 3:16), and of these I claim to be. No one among them can need to be cleansed from all his filthiness, and from all his idols, and to be saved from all his uncleannesses, more than I need it. I do, therefore, regard myself as an heir to the good here promised.

"**And they shall be My people, and I will be their God: and I will give them one heart, and one way, that they may fear Me for ever, for the good of them and their children after them: and I will make an everlasting covenant with them, that I will not turn away from them to do good; but I will put My fear in their hearts, that they shall not depart from Me**" (Jeremiah 32:38-40). Should it again be said that these promises were made to the Jews only, I utterly deny that any natural descendant of Abraham has any right, title, or inheritance, in these exceeding great and precious promises, which does not equally belong to me as a disciple of Christ. Should it be said, that these promises are connected with the literal return of the Jews to their own land, I reply, that God has said, "**no good thing will He withhold from them that walk uprightly**" (Psalms 84:11); and that "**He that spared not His Son, but delivered**

Him up for us all, how shall He not with Him also freely give us all things?" (Romans 8:32). And since no lost sinner more needs the good here promised than myself, I urge my humble claim through Christ to all the good here brought to view, and regard it as my inheritance.

Again, it is said in Jeremiah 31:31-33, **"Behold, the days come, saith the LORD, that I will make a new covenant with the house of Israel, and with the house of Judah: not according to the covenant that I made with their fathers in the day that I took them by the hand to bring them out of the land of Egypt; which My covenant they brake, although I was an husband unto them, saith the LORD: but this shall be the covenant that I will make with the house of Israel; After those days, saith the LORD, I will put My law in their inward parts, and write it in their hearts; and will be their God, and they shall be My people."**

This is the same pledge of being brought to love God with all the heart, soul, mind and strength; and of this pledge and benefit of the new covenant I cannot be deprived; for of this new covenant Christ is the mediator, as we are told by Paul, in his Epistle to the Hebrews; so that to fulfill this new covenant is the very thing which Christ came to do. His own blood Christ Himself called the **"blood of the new testament"** (Mark 14:24), or covenant; and Paul said of himself and his fellow apostles, **"God hath made us able ministers of the new testament; not of the letter that killeth, but of the spirit that giveth life"** (2 Corinthians 3:6). This new covenant, therefore, which puts God's law in the hearts of His people, and by that means takes away their sins, should be regarded as the great and glorious theme of them that preach in the name of Christ.

It is the fulfillment of this covenant which Christ has in view, when He says, **"Blessed are they that do hunger and thirst after righteousness, for they shall be filled"** (Matthew 5:6). **"He that cometh to Me** shall never hunger; and he that believeth on Me shall never thirst. As the living Father hath sent Me, and I live by the Father: so he that eateth Me, even he shall live by Me" (John 6:35, 57). "**Ask, and ye shall receive; seek, and ye shall find; knock, and it shall be opened to you. For every one that asketh receiveth; and he that seeketh findeth; and to him that knocketh it shall be opened. If a son ask bread of any of you that is a father, will he give him a stone? or if he ask a fish, will he for a fish give him a serpent? Or if he ask an egg, will he offer him a scorpion? If ye then, being evil, know how to give good things to your children: how much more shall your Father which is in heaven give good things to them that ask Him?**" (Luke 11:9-13). That these promises refer to the blessings of the new covenant, I infer from the fact that there is no good which we so much need, as to have God's law put into our hearts, so that we may truly love Him "**with all our heart, and with all our soul**" (Matthew 22:37; Deuteronomy 10:12). And since He has made this covenant, and sent Christ to be the Mediator of it, and has thus assured us of His utmost readiness to give every good thing, I see the way wide open for Christians to be "**cleansed from all unrighteousness**" (1 John 1:9).

It is in the fulfillment of this new covenant that that will be accomplished for which our Saviour taught us to pray, "**Thy kingdom come. Thy will be done in earth, as it is in heaven**" (Matthew 6:10). For when God's law is put into the hearts of His people, so that they truly love Him "**with all the heart, and with all the soul**" (Matthew 22:37), then His kingdom is come within them, and then His will is done in them on earth as it is done in heaven.

To the blessings of this new covenant, we may also apply other great and precious promises of our Saviour. "**All things, whatsoever ye shall ask in prayer, believing, ye shall receive**" (Matthew 21:22). "**Hitherto have ye asked nothing in My name: ask, and ye shall re-**

ceive, that your joy may be full." (John 16:24). When the Christian finds his sins taken away, and the new covenant fulfilled in Him, so that he does "**love God with all his heart, and with all his soul**," then "**his joy is full**," and it never can be full until then. Accordingly, John, in writing his Epistle, says, "**these things write we unto you, that your joy may be full**" (1 John 1:4).

And what does he then write, to give Christians fullness of joy? Why, that "**the blood of Jesus Christ cleanseth us from all sin**" (1 John 1:7); that "**if we confess our sins, he is faithful and just to forgive us our sins, and to cleanse us from all unrighteousness**" (1 John 1:9); that "**He was manifested to take away our sins**" (1 John 3:5); and that "**whosoever abideth in Him sinneth not**" (1 John 3:6). These are the very things to give the Christian fullness of joy, and nothing short of these can do it.

One more passage I will now quote, and then on this point I shall have done. It is that passage, in relation to which Paul says to the Corinthians, "**Having therefore these promises, dearly beloved, let us cleanse ourselves from all filthiness of the flesh and spirit, perfecting holiness in the fear of God**" (2 Corinthians 7:1). The passage is this: "**For ye are the temple of the living God; as God hath said, I will dwell in them, and walk in them; and I will be their God, and they shall be My people. Wherefore come out from among them, and be ye separate, saith the Lord, and touch not the unclean thing; and I will receive you, and will be a Father unto you, and ye shall be my sons and daughters, saith the Lord Almighty**" (2 Corinthians 6:16-18).

Here, in my view, the apostle means to teach, that, in the promises, "**I will dwell in them, and walk in them; and I will be their God, and they shall be my people**" (2 Corinthians 6:16), there is the promise of being cleansed from all filthiness of the flesh and spirit, and of perfecting holiness in the fear of God. If, then, we can find a way to secure to us the fulfillment of these exceeding great and precious promises, we shall, as it seems to me, attain to the highest possible good. I shall, therefore, now inquire,

Second,

2. How shall we gain the fulfillment of God's promises?

On this point I remark, that there is a passage which has served me as a key to unlock the rich treasures of God's Word; and which, for some years, has been opening to me more and more "**the riches of the glory of Christ's inheritance in the saints**" (Ephesians 1:18), and which has done very much to bring me where I am, "**by the grace of God**" today. It is found in 2 Corinthians 1:20: "**For all the promises of God in Him (that is, in Christ) are yea, and in Him Amen, unto the glory of God by us.**" By this I understand that while no promise of God is ever fulfilled to us, except for Christ's sake, we may have the fulfillment of every promise, for the fulfillment of which we trust in Christ; and that when we trust in Christ, and receive for His sake the fulfillment of God's promises, God is glorified by us. Take, then, the promise, "**I, even I, am He that blotteth out thy transgressions for mine own sake, and will not remember thy sins**" (Isaiah 43:25). To whom is that promise fulfilled? To him, and to him only, who trusts in Christ, to have it fulfilled to him for Christ's sake. Such an one always receives pardon, and none else.

Take now the promises, "**I will sprinkle clean water upon you, and make you clean from all your filthiness; and from all your idols will I cleanse you, and I will save you from all your uncleannesses**" (Ezekiel 36:25, 29); "**the very God of peace who hath called you in faith to sanctify you wholly; and to preserve your whole spirit and soul and body blameless unto the coming of our Lord Jesus Christ**" (1 Thessalonians 5:23); and to whom are these promises fulfilled? *Like the promises pledging forgiveness of sins, they are all yea and amen in*

Christ, to the glory of God by us, so that when we come to Christ, and trust in Him, to have these promises fulfilled to us for His sake, God will glorify Himself, by sprinkling clean water upon us, by cleansing us from all our filthiness and from all our idols, and by sanctifying us wholly, and **"preserving our whole spirit, and soul, and body, blameless unto the coming of our Lord Jesus Christ."**

Through the *promises* of God, then, we cleanse ourselves from all filthiness of the flesh and spirit, and perfect holiness in the fear of God, when we believe in the Lord Jesus Christ, that these promises will be fulfilled to us for His sake. Herein, it seems to me, there is, in these last days, a great departure from the faith—and that when the church of Christ will learn to cleanse herself from all filthiness of the flesh and spirit, and to perfect holiness in the fear of God, by trusting in Christ for the fulfillment of those exceeding great and precious promises which pledge to her salvation from all her uncleanness, **"she will put on her beautiful garments"** (Isaiah 52:1), and **"arise and shine; her light having come, and the glory of the LORD having arisen upon her"** (Isaiah 60:1).

And now, dear brother, I will look directly to your questions. You have already had abundant reply as to the question, whether men are, or may be holy in this life. While I believe that there is little holiness in the world, I believe there is abundant provision made in God's grace, by which Christians **"may stand perfect and complete in all the will of God"** (Colossians 4:12); and I believe that in the days of Paul, Peter and John, this grace was fully available, through faith in Christ, for the fulfillment of God's promise —and no less so now, to all who will in the same way avail themselves of it.

As it respects the martyrs, I believe that no man ever became a martyr for Christ, who was not actually cleansed from all sin; because, the giving up of the whole world, and life itself, for Christ's sake, fully evince that such an one must have loved Christ with his whole and undivided heart, and must, therefore, have been free from sin. Men may have become martyrs to other things, with no regard to Christ, as millions have done to the mad passions of men; but no man, in my apprehension, ever could become a martyr for Christ's sake, whose heart was not purified, and filled with love to Christ. I believe, therefore, that every real gospel martyr was cleansed from sin, before he left the world.

In modern times, many godly men have seemed not fully to apprehend all the riches of the grace of God, and have maintained, that no Christian ever did on earth "**cleanse himself from all filthiness of the flesh and spirit, and perfect holiness in the fear of God**" (2 Corinthians 7:1). *But if a man can be cleansed from sin, by faith in Christ for the fulfillment of God's promises, a moment before death, why not a day, a year, or twenty or fifty years?*

You asked my views, respecting the general character of those who have embraced the doctrine of entire sanctification in this life. I answer, I have no doubt that some, professing a belief in this doctrine, have been licentious—so have some who profess to believe in the doctrine of the new birth, but I do not see that in either case, their licentiousness is in any sense chargeable, upon the doctrine which they profess to believe. I can no more conceive that a man should become licentious as a direct consequence of trusting in Christ to be kept by the grace of God from all sin, than that a man should sink to hell, in consequence of trusting in Christ to save him from hell. In either case, in my apprehension, the evil must result from want of faith in Christ, and not from the exercise of it.

And now, as to the greater safety of those that fear always—I answer, that he who trusts in Christ to be kept from all sin, is the man, and the only man, that does fear always. He not only fears, but *knows* that he never shall, in any instance, keep himself, and therefore always flies to Christ; while he who does not fear always, does not trust in Christ, and therefore falls into sin. I do therefore most fully believe, that he who fears always, is most safe, provided his fears are sufficiently great to drive him to the Lord, in Whom alone he has righteousness and strength. This fear hath no torment—it is a sweet reliance on Christ.

I do not, therefore, think that any man's absurdities, irregularities, inconsistencies, or crimes, are in any sense chargeable upon the doctrine which I advocate. The more precious the coin, the more desirable the counterfeit, to a wicked man. That the blessed doctrine of being kept from all sin by faith in Christ, will be counterfeited by unholy men, for licentious purposes, I have not a doubt; but shall I, therefore, cast away the coin—the most precious that ever fell down to lost man, from the exhaustless mint of heaven! No, my brother. The Word of God assures me that my Redeemer was "**called JESUS: because He should save His people from their sins**" (Matthew 1:21); "**manifested to take away our sins and that whosoever abideth in Him sinneth not**" (1 John 3:5, 6); and to that Saviour I must cleave as with the grasp of death; for I see a moment's safety no where but under the shadow of His wing. "**I will therefore say of the LORD, He is my refuge and my fortress: my God; in Him will I trust. Surely He shall deliver me from the snare of the fowler, and from the noisome pestilence. He shall cover me with His feathers, and under His wings will I trust: His truth in the fulfillment of His own exceeding great and precious promises shall be my shield and buckler**" (Psalms 91:2-4; 2 Peter 1:4).

And now, brother, I believe there are those who do embrace this great salvation fully, so that their characters are formed by it, and who can say, "**The life that I live here in the flesh I live by the faith of the Son of God, who loved me, and gave Himself for me**" (Galatians 2:20); and I do believe that they are not only decidedly, but eminently, more meek and heavenly than any other class of men. I ought here to say, however that nothing, in my apprehension, is holiness, which falls short of

31

the fulfillment of that promise, "**The LORD thy God will circumcise thine heart, and the heart of thy seed, to love the LORD thy God with** *all thy heart*, **and with all thy soul**" (Deuteronomy 30:6). The child of God is not, in my apprehension, a "**whited sepulchre**" (Matthew 23:27). Holiness is "**the righteousness of the law fulfilled in us**" (Romans 8:4). With any view of sanctification which does not make it consist in "**loving God with all the heart, and our neighbor as ourselves**" (Luke 10:27), I have no fellowship. If a man expresses to me his belief that, through the operations of the Holy Spirit upon his heart, received by faith in Christ for the fulfillment of God's promises, he is enabled "**to love God with all his heart, and his neighbor as himself**" (Luke 10:27); inasmuch as I know that God has promised "**to circumcise his heart, to love the Lord his God with all his heart, and with all his soul**" (Deuteronomy 30:6). I have no right to doubt that the promises of God are thus fulfilled in him, unless I see that in his life he does depart from "**the right way of the Lord**" (2 Peter 2:15), as it is revealed in His holy Word. But "**to the law and to the testimony: if they speak not according to this word, it is because there is no light in them**" (Isaiah 8:20).

I am fully aware, however, that there are those who claim to be "**perfect in Christ Jesus**" (Colossians 1:28), who do fall into gross mistakes on this very point; and in this way do, in a very grievous manner, cause "**the way of truth to be evil spoken of**" (Romans 14:16). By laying aside the plain written Word of God, as the rule, and the only rule by which they are to govern their faith, and try their feelings, and form their opinions, and shape all their conduct, and taking up the belief that the Holy Spirit so dwells in them that they need not resort to the Bible as their only guide, but may follow whatever impulse arises within them, they step at once on the broad ground of fanaticism, and become what Christ would have been, if He had, at the suggestion of Satan, thrown Himself from the pinnacle of the temple—tempters of God.

While God has promised me, in His Word, everything requisite to meet all the real necessities of my being, even to the full accomplishment of my highest good, both on earth and in heaven, He has nowhere given me license to transgress either His physical or moral laws, with the expectation that He will meet a necessity that I thus presumptuously create. If I were to leap from an eminence, with the expectation that God would save me from death by counteracting the law of gravitation, or by giving me wings; or, if I were voluntarily to abstain from food, with the expectation that God would preserve my life without eating; or venture to sea in a leaky ship, with the confidence that God would save me from a watery grave, I should be tempting God, by a willful transgression of physical law. I have no right to expect any miraculous assurance before hand, as He did to Moses, that He will be with me in a miraculous manner.

No more am I to transgress moral precepts, by casting myself into the way o f temptation unnecessarily, thinking that God will there keep me from being overcome; or by doing an act which God's Word plainly forbids, through the presumption that the Holy Spirit guides me to it, and that it, therefore, is not sin. I know there are those who have ventured on this ground, and by so doing, have brought amazing reproach on Christ and His cause. I am not to "**believe every spirit, but try the spirits whether they are of God**" (1 John 4:1). But by what rule am I to try every spirit? Plainly by the revealed Word, I have no other rule, and I need no other. If I feel an impulse, then to do a thing contrary to the plain Word of God, I need not mistake the source from whence such an impulse comes. I know the devil is the originator of such an impulse, just as infallibly as though I were to see his snaky head, or his forked tongue, or his glaring eyes, or hear the hissings of his hellish throat. I know there are those who are accustomed to say, "Whatever the Lord should tell me, I would do." But I know the Lord will never tell them to do a thing contrary to the Bible; and when led to anything of this sort, they are surely led by Satan.

Besides, I do not expect to influence the conduct of my fellow men, unless I can show them good and sufficient reasons for the course I wish them to pursue. Much more may I expect, that where the Holy Ghost would lead me, He will show me the best reasons for following Him; and for these reasons, I am to look into that Word which He has inspired.

From this very error of following impulses instead of the Word of God, have grown up all the inconsistencies, absurdities, irregularities, and in some cases, as I do not doubt, licentious practices of some, called Perfectionists. Instead of cleaving closely to the Word of God, making it their only rule of life, writing it on their hearts, and setting it always, "**as a frontlet between their eyes**" (Deuteronomy 6:8), they have imbibed the idea that the Holy Spirit so dwells in them, as to be an infallible guide, without any reference to God's plainly revealed will. And when a man steps on that ground, he may well expect, like him who went down from Jerusalem to Jericho, and fell among thieves, to find himself wounded, stripped of his raiment, and left, at least, half dead. He throws himself defenseless among mortal foes; for the Word of God should be to him sword and shield. He might as well cast away rudder, and compass, and chart, and quadrant, and chronometer in mid-ocean, and expect God to guide him to his desired haven. Or as well, wandering among pit-falls in black midnight, cast away his only lamp, and think to walk safely by faith. The Holy Spirit has indeed been given to guide us into all truth, but all the truth we need to know is in the Bible; and all the guidance we need, is to a right understanding and practice of what the Bible contains.

But when God has plainly revealed to me that He is ready "**to sprinkle clean water upon me, and make me clean from all my filthiness, and from all my idols, to cleanse me, and to save me from all** my uncleanness when I inquire of Him to do it for me" (Ezekiel 36:25,29); and when He has sworn that He will grant unto me, that "I being delivered out of the hand of my enemies, may serve Him without fear, in holiness and righteousness before Him, all the days of my life, and has raised up Christ, an horn of salvation for me, to perform that covenant and oath" (Luke 1:74, 75, 69, 72, 73), and has assured me that "all the promises of God in Christ are yea, and in Him Amen, unto the glory of God by me" (2 Corinthians 1:20); do I follow impulses and not the Bible, when I fully trust in Christ, that these promises and this oath of God will be fulfilled to me for Christ's sake? Can I be in danger of going astray by thus cleaving to my own horn of salvation, whom God has raised up for me, and by just trusting in Him, that He will perform for me the very thing that He came to do?

On this point, my brother, my heart is oppressed, and labors for words to express its gushing emotions. I seem, to myself, to be standing in a position whence two ways diverge. In the one, I see a class of persons walking, who cry out, "Away with the Sabbath days, ordinances and the written Word of God—away with all laws and rules of conduct, both human and divine. We need no law, no rule of faith or practice, no means of grace, no private devotion and communion with our Father in secret, no domestic altars, no earnest, wrestling prayer, and faithful, persevering effort, to convert a lost world to God. We dwell in Christ and He in us, and therefore we cannot sin; and whatever impulse we feel, we know to be the influence of the Holy Ghost, who cannot err, and we may therefore safely follow wherever such an influence leads."

In the ears of such I should cry out at the top of my voice, Danger, danger, danger! Beware, beware! Go not in such a path! Avoid it—pass by it—turn from it and pass away! Here are the class of men called Perfectionists. Can I walk with them upon such ground? Not a hair's breadth. So far from forsaking the commandments and ordinances of the *Lord*, my Bible tells me to "**submit myself to every ordinance of man even, for the Lord's sake**" (1 Peter 2:13), that "*the powers that be are ordained of God*" (Romans 13:1), and that "**whosoever, therefore, resisteth the power, resisteth the ordinance of God**" (Romans 13:2).

With such men, on such subjects, I have, I can have, no sympathy. I believe there are some truly converted souls who fall into these errors, and are dreadfully led astray. I believe that others take up these notions, in whose hearts no fear of God ever for a moment had a place, and follow them out into all manner of licentious and criminal excess. Such become the most perfect and accomplished servants of Satan that he ever raises up to do his work. I cannot conceive that the arch-deceiver can ever originate a worse set of principles than these. I could as soon sympathize with any form of infidelity that ever cursed the earth.

But on the other hand, and in the other path, I see a multitude of professed believers walking, who through fear of going astray, dare not believe God when He tells them, "**I will cleanse you from all your filthiness, and from all your idols**" (Ezekiel 36:25), and when He swears to them that He "**will grant unto them, that they being delivered out of the hand of their enemies might serve Him without fear, in holiness and righteousness before Him all the days of their life**" (Luke 1:74-75).

Can I sympathize with the unbelief of such? I believe that it is their privilege, and my privilege, so to "**abide in Christ, that we sin not**" (1 John 3:6)—that "**the work of such righteousness is peace; the effect of such righteousness, quietness and assurance for ever, and that all who will thus believe in Christ, may find in Him a peaceful habitation, a sure dwelling, a quiet resting place**" (Isaiah 32:17, 18).

I long to have God's people know and enjoy their high privilege of thus abiding in Christ, for I fully believe that it will redound to the highest degree to God's honor and their good. This view of sanctification, I claim, has nothing to do with the essential element of what is termed

Perfectionism. Their name and their principles I utterly disavow, and declare to the world that no man has a right to charge them upon me.

But when I look around upon the professed followers of my Saviour, and see how little they know, apparently, and how little they seem to enjoy, of this great salvation of our God, I feel like lifting the prayer:

"Every weary, wandering spirit,
Guide into Thy perfect peace."

And when I see how many, bearing the name of Christ, seem wandering among doubts and fears, and groping in thick darkness at noon day, falling before spiritual enemies whom they know not how to vanquish, and weeping over the repeated commission of sins which they know not how to overcome, I long to say to such:

"Watchman!
let thy wandering cease,
Hie thee to thy quiet home,
Traveller!
Lo! the Prince of Peace—
Lo! the Son of God is come!"

Look no longer, like scattered, unbelieving Israel, for a Saviour yet to come. Say, with believing Zacharias, **"Blessed be the Lord God of Israel; for He hath visited and redeemed His people, and hath raised up an horn of salvation to perform His promised mercy, His covenant, His oath; to deliver us out of the hand of our enemies, and to grant unto us that we may serve Him without fear, in holiness and righteousness before Him, all the days of our life"** (Luke 1:68-69, 72-75).

You ask me, finally, concerning myself. Here, dear brother, I speak with unfeigned diffidence. I love to look at my Saviour, and to hold Him forth in all His fullness to my needy, perishing fellow men. But in myself, aside from what the grace of God has done, and shall do for me, I find nothing but the dark and perfect lineaments of Beelzebub, the prince of devils. I speak sincerely, my brother. I know that if God should withdraw His grace from me, and leave me to myself, there is not a sin within the reach of my powers, which I would not instantly commit and practice for ever.

And now, having told you what I think of myself, to my own shame, permit me to tell you what I think of the grace of God, to His praise. **"God has promised to dwell in me, and walk in me; and be my God"** (2 Corinthians 6:16); and this I consider a pledge of every possible good which He can give me. **"Having therefore such promises,"** I expect, by trusting in Christ, that they will be fulfilled to me for His sake, **"to be cleansed from all filthiness of the flesh and spirit, and to perfect holiness in the fear of God"** (2 Corinthians 7:1). My God has sworn that He will grant me, that I, being delivered out of the hand of my enemies, may serve Him without fear, in holiness and righteousness before Him all the days of my life; and He has raised up Jesus Christ to be my horn of salvation, to perform to me this mercy promised to our fathers, to remember this holy covenant, this oath which He sware. I do therefore expect, through the strength and faithfulness of my Lord Jesus Christ, in performing to me this holy covenant and oath of God, to be delivered out of the hand of my enemies, and to serve God without fear, in holiness and righteousness before Him, all the days of my life. I expect that He, according to His own promise, will be faithful to sanctify me wholly, and to preserve my whole spirit, and soul, and body, blameless, unto the coming of our Lord Jesus Christ. In myself, I am nothing but a miserable, lost sinner; but in my Saviour, **"dwelleth all the fullness of the Godhead bodily;"** and He has made me **"complete in Him"** (Colossians 2:9-10). I therefore expect **"to abide in Him, and whosoever abideth in Him sinneth not"** (1 John 3:6).

And now, my brother, as to what I expect to preach, I have only to say, that I expect to uncover to my fellow men, just so far and just so long as my God shall enable me, "**this fountain which has been opened to the house of David and to the inhabitants of Jerusalem for sin and for uncleanness**" (Zechariah 13:1). I expect to do all in my power to make my fellow men acquainted with the "**holy covenant of our God, and the oath which He sware, that He will grant unto us, that we, being delivered out of the hand of our enemies, may serve Him without fear, in holiness and righteousness before Him, all the days of our lives; and that Christ is our horn of salvation to perform this covenant; this oath of a covenant-keeping God**" (Luke 1:72-75; 69); that this and every other "**promise of God is yea and Amen in Christ, unto the glory of God by us**" (2 Corinthians 1:20). "**That He who hath called them is faithful, to sanctify them wholly; to preserve their whole spirit and soul and body be preserved blameless unto the coming of our Lord Jesus Christ**" (1 Thessalonians 5:24, 23). "**That Christ gave Himself for us, that He might sanctify and cleanse us with the washing of water by the Word, that He might present us to Himself, a glorious church, not having spot, or wrinkle, or any such thing; but that we should be holy and without blemish**" (Ephesians 5:25-27); and that they have only, like Paul to "**believe God, that it shall be even as it was told them**" (Acts 27:25); and, like Abraham, to "**stagger not at the promise of God through unbelief; but to be strong in faith, giving glory to God, being fully persuaded that, what He had promised, He was able also to perform**" (Romans 4:20-21); and, like Sarah, to "**judge Him faithful who had promised**" (Hebrews 11:11); and by placing this confidence in their Saviour, they shall so receive the fulfillment of "**God's exceeding great and precious promises as to become partakers of the divine nature, having escaped the corruption that is in the world through lust**" (2 Peter 1:4); that "**having these promises and this faith in Christ for their fulfillment,**

they shall cleanse themselves from all filthiness of the flesh and spirit, perfecting holiness in the fear of God" (2 Corinthians 7:1).

This, my brother, I regard as the glory, the crowning excellency of the gospel, the brightest star in the whole firmament of revealed truth; and with my Saviour's permission, I expect to point my fellow men to this Day Star of hope, until the hand that points them is given to the worms. It is, to my soul, a fountain of living waters, a wellspring of life, and I expect to say to my fellow men, "**Ho, every one that thirsteth, come ye to the waters, and he that hath no money; come ye, buy, and eat; yea, come, buy wine and milk without money and without price**" (Isaiah 55:1); and cease not, until the lips that are allowed the high privilege of uttering such an invitation, can speak no more.

And now, my dear brother; you have my whole heart laid open without reserve; and to God I commit myself, and His truth, and the cause of the Saviour, dearer to me than life. "**Now unto Him that is able to keep you from falling, and to present you faultless before the presence of His glory with exceeding joy, to the only wise God our Saviour, be glory and majesty, dominion and power, both now and forever. Amen**" (Jude 1:24-25).

Your servant in the gospel,
CHARLES FITCH

Letter to the Presbytery of Newark

by Charles Fitch,
Found in *Guide to Christian Perfection*,
Vol. 1, No. 10, April, 1840, pp. 217-234.

Dear Brethren:

After being made acquainted with my views and feelings on the subject of sanctification, you have passed a resolution declaring them to be important and dangerous error, and admonishing me to preach them no more. I must therefore say, brethren, and I hope to do it with all meekness, and humility, and lowliness of heart, that I cannot regard your admonition; and for the following reasons.

REASON ONE

1. It is now several years, since, after a season of spiritual gloom and sadness, I came fully to the conclusion, that there was something in the religion of Jesus Christ, to which I had been a stranger. I had seen myself to be a sinner before God, richly deserving His everlasting indignation. I had seen that God would be holy, just and good, and worthy of universal and eternal adoration, while punishing me with everlasting destruction from His presence and from the glory of His power. I had also seen in Christ a Saviour, who, after atoning for all mankind on the cross, was able, on the merits of that atonement, to save to the uttermost all that come to God by Him; and on that Saviour I had cast myself as my only hope, and trusted in Him, and Him only, as my Deliverer from the wrath of God.

Trusting thus in Him—my crucified Saviour—for my salvation, I was for a time filled with great joy and peace in believing, and went on my way rejoicing. But years passed away, and to these lively emotions of joy in the Lord, I had been almost an entire stranger, except for a short season immediately succeeding my first conversion to Christ—when I did taste in a good degree, the peace which those are sure to find, who come with a heart penitent for sin, and trust in the merits of a crucified Saviour for pardon and everlasting life. But I had come now to the full conviction, that my religious state was very far from what it ought to be. This arose partly from what I had learned in the Bible respecting **"the riches of the glory of this mystery which is Christ in us, the hope of glory"** (Colossians 1:27); **"the peace of God, which passeth all understanding, keeping the heart and mind of the Christian through Christ Jesus"** (Philippians 4:7), and **"the joy unspeakable and full of glory to be found in Him, Whom not having seen, we love; in Whom, though now we see Him not, yet believing, we rejoice"** (1 Peter 1:8); and partly from what I learned about that time of the experience of some Christians, to which experience I knew myself to be a stranger.

I came then to a settled determination to know, with the help of God, more of spiritual things. Since that time, which is now some years, I have, as never before, **"cried after knowledge, and lifted up my voice for understanding, seeking her as silver, and searching for her as for hid treasures that I might understand the fear of the LORD, and find the knowledge of God"** (Proverbs 2:3-5).

I have sought for spiritual bread and for the water of life, with an earnestness which I know I have never felt for any of the possessions of this world. I have sought these in the Bible, in the experience of eminent Christians who have gone to their reward, and in the writings of living Christians who seem to know most of spiritual things. I have sought them in personal conversation with those who seemed to know most of the deep things of God, and I have sought them on my knees, with many tears, and with earnest wrestlings in the name of Christ for the teachings of the Holy Ghost. For a long time there was no definite blessing that I had in my mind as the object of pursuit, except that I might have more of the Holy Ghost, and be far better prepared than I had ever been to live to the glory of God.

But I was made acquainted, in the providence of God, with some of those Christians who believe that it is the privilege of all disciples of Christ to be, through the **"great God and our Saviour Jesus Christ who hath loved us and gave Himself for us, redeemed from all iniquity, and purified unto Himself a peculiar people, zealous of good works"** (Titus 2:13-14); and we **"through the blood of the everlasting covenant to be made perfect in every good work to do His will, by His working in us that which is well-pleasing in His sight, through Jesus Christ"** (Hebrews 13:20-21)—to be **"sanctified wholly, and to have their whole spirit and soul and body be preserved blameless unto the coming of our Lord Jesus Christ through the faithfulness of Him who hath called them"** (1 Thessalonians 5:23-24)—to be **"cleansed from all filthiness of the flesh and spirit, and to perfect holiness in the fear of God"** (2 Corinthians 7:1); **"through the promises of God which are all yea and Amen in Christ, unto the glory of God by us"** (2 Corinthians 1:20), and thus through the **"exceeding great and precious promises to be made partakers of the divine nature, having escaped the corruption that is in the world through lust"** (2 Peter 1:4).

When I first knew this class of Christians, and first read their writings, I was greatly opposed to their views of truth, and from what I had learned of the mistakes and excesses of some who had professed to hold this truth, and to enjoy the experience of it, I was led to regard the whole subject with very great aversion. But I have learned that truth is not to be held accountable for excesses into which these mistakes may lead them, nor for the sins of those who hold the truth in unrighteousness.

While I was thus crying after knowledge, and lifting up my voice for understanding, the Lord began to teach me more and more of the love of Christ, so that I was not only restored to my first love, but made to know, in my own experience, that "**the path of the just is as the shining light, which shineth more and more unto the perfect day**" (Proverbs 4:18), and that whoso "**followeth Christ shall not walk in darkness, but shall have the light of life**" (John 8:12). "**The peace of God, which passeth all understanding, keeping the heart and the mind through Christ Jesus**" (Philippians 4:7), and the "**joy unspeakable and full of glory**" (1 Peter 1:8), of which the Bible speaks, became realities to my mind; and I had learned the blessed truth, that "**all the promises of God in Christ are yea, and in Him Amen, unto the glory of God by us**" (2 Corinthians 1:20); that it is the Christian's privilege, by trusting in Christ for the fulfillment of the promises, to enjoy the fulfillment of every one of them, just as the awakened sinner has fulfilled to him the promise of pardon, when, and only when he believes for this on Christ.

I had then inquired what has God promised, and what is He willing to do for me, if I believe for it in Christ. I examined the Bible with this principle in view, and found that God has said, "**I will instruct thee and teach thee in the way thou shalt go: I will guide thee with mine eye**" (Psalms 32:8). This promise I knew to be yea and amen in Christ unto the glory of God by me, and I therefore prayed and trusted in Christ that God would instruct me, and teach me in the way that I should go, and guide me with His eye, "**into all truth**" (John 16:13), respecting the doctrine of "**sanctification**" (1 Peter 1:2).

When I read the promises on this subject, I found them full and explicit. "**I *will* circumcise thine heart, and the heart of thy seed, to** love the LORD thy God with all thine heart, and with all thy soul" (Deuteronomy 30:6). "I *will* sprinkle clean water upon you, and *make* you clean: from all your filthiness, and from all your idols, will I cleanse you. I *will* take away the stony heart out of your flesh, and I *will* give you an heart of flesh, and I *will* put My spirit within you, and cause you to walk in My statutes, and ye shall keep My judgments, and do them, and I will also save you from all your uncleannesses" (Ezekiel 36:25-27, 29). And "I *will* make an everlasting covenant with you, that I will not turn away from you, to do you good; but I will put My fear in your hearts, that ye shall not depart from Me" (Jeremiah 32:40). And "this is the covenant that I will make with the house of Israel after those days, saith the Lord, I will put My laws into their hearts, and in their minds will I write them; and their sins and iniquities will I remember no more" (Hebrews 10:16,17).

I also found that Christ, our Redeemer, was called Jesus because "He would save His people from their sins" (Matthew 1:21); that "He was manifested to take away our sins; and that whosoever abideth in Him sinneth not" (1 John 3:5, 6).

I also found many other Scriptures equally full and explicit. But after all this, unbelief triumphed in my mind, and I could not see how it should ever be to me reality in this life, that "the blood of Jesus Christ should cleanse me from all sin" (1 John 1:7). But as I prayed more and more for the teachings of God's Spirit, and searched after the truth, I found that "If we confess our sins, He is faithful and just to forgive us our sins, and to cleanse us from all unrighteousness" (1 John 1:9). He is as faithful to cleanse us as He is to forgive.

I found also that Christ was "raised up an horn of salvation," "to perform the mercy promised to the fathers, and to remember God's holy covenant, the oath which He sware to our father Abraham, that He would grant unto us, that we being delivered out of the hand of

our enemies might serve Him without fear, in holiness and righteousness before Him, all the days of our life" (Luke 1:69, 72-75).

When I inquired why are not these promises, so rich and full, made good to God's people, I saw that as they were yea and amen only in Christ, they were to be fulfilled, like the promises pledging the pardon of sin, to those, and only those, who believed in Christ for their fulfillment. This led me to see that if I would be cleansed from all unrighteousness, as well as have my sins forgiven, I must believe for that cleansing, in Him of whom it is said, **"If we confess our sins, he is faithful and just to forgive us our sins, and to cleanse us from all unrighteousness"** (1 John 1:9).

On Him, therefore, I now endeavored oftentimes to cast myself, by trusting simply in His faithfulness, that He would cleanse me from all unrighteousness. But I had yet no evidence on which I could rest a belief that I was thus cleansed. I went on thus, continuing to pray, and endeavoring to trust in Christ, for this cleansing gift of the Holy Spirit, desiring above all things to be cleansed from all unrighteousness. In this state of mind, I had one day taken my Testament, and a little work on "Christian Perfection" by Fletcher, and given myself up to reading, meditation, and prayer on this subject. I opened Fletcher at the following passage:

"My heart strings groan
with deep complaint—
My flesh lies panting,
Lord, for Thee,
And every limb, and every joint,
Stretches for perfect purity.

"But if the Lord be pleased to come softly to thy help; if He make an end of thy corruptions by helping thee gently to sink to unknown depths of meekness; if He drown the indwelling man of sin by baptizing, by plunging him into an abyss of humility; do not find fault with the simplicity of His method, the plainness of His appearing and the commonness of His prescription. Nature, like Naaman, is full of prejudices. She expects that Christ will come to make her clean, with as much ado and pomp and bustle, as the Syrian general looked for, when **"he was wroth, and said, Behold, I thought, He will surely come out to me, and stand, and call on his God, and strike his hand over the place, and recover the leper"** (2 Kings 5:11). Christ frequently goes a much plainer way to work: and by this means disconcerts all our preconceived notions and schemes of deliverance. **"Learn of Me to be meek and lowly in heart: and thou shall find rest unto thy soul"** (Matthew 11:29), the sweet rest of Christian perfection, of perfect humility, resignation and meekness. If thou wilt absolutely come to mount Zion in a triumphal chariot, or make thine entrance into the new Jerusalem upon a prancing horse, thou art likely never to come there. Leave, then, all thy worldly misconceptions behind, and humbly follow thy King, who makes His entry into the typical Jerusalem, **"meek and lowly, riding upon an ass, yea, upon a colt, the foal of an ass"** (Matthew 21:5)."

These remarks were particularly blessed to me. It seemed to me, indeed, a most delightful thing to sink into the meek and lowly spirit of the blessed Saviour. I had before been laboring to rise above my sins, and thus leave them; now I felt willing to sink below them, into a depth of humility, where the proud, unhumbled spirit of sin would not be willing to follow, and it seemed a delightful thing to sink in the arms of my Saviour, below the reach of all my spiritual foes, when I had long been seeking in vain to escape them, by soaring above.

I felt then in my spirit a most sweet and heavenly sinking into the arms of my Redeemer, such as I had not before experienced, and it was followed by a calm, unruffled, blissful peace in Christ—such as I need not attempt to describe to those who have tasted it, and such as I cannot describe to the comprehension of those whose hearts have never felt it.

It was attended with such a full and delightful submission in all things to the will of God; such a joy of heart, in the thought of being for life, and for death, and for ever, altogether at God's disposal; such a gladness in giving up earth in all its possessions and pleasures for Christ's sake; such an overflowing of humble, penitential, grateful love to my Redeemer; such a satisfaction in the thought of having Him as my only everlasting portion; such praise to His name that I might possess Him as the portion of my soul for ever; such full-hearted and unshrinking confidence in all His promises, and such a readiness to do and suffer all things, even to the laying down of life for His name's sake, that I felt constrained to say, this is purity of heart.

I knew that nothing but the Holy Spirit could ever fill such a heart as mine had been, with such feelings as these, and I therefore believed it to be the work of the Holy Spirit, cleansing my heart from the defilement of sin. I know that some persons are ready to say, all this may be the delusion of Satan, leading you to think of yourself more highly than you ought to think. But I do not think that the devil ever yet attempted to fill the heart of any man with the love of God.

Christ said to His disciples, "**I will pray the Father, and He shall give you another Comforter, that He may abide with you for ever; even the Spirit of truth; whom the world cannot receive, because it seeth Him not, neither knoweth Him:** *but ye know Him*; **for He dwelleth with you, and shall be in you.**" (John 14:16-17).

The true disciple, therefore, will know the Comforter. I know that the feelings I have now described were a blessed reality; that there was nothing left in my will or affections in opposition to them, and I do therefore believe that the Saviour gave me to know, at that moment, something of the blessedness of being redeemed from all iniquity, and purified unto Himself. For some length of time I continued in that blessed state of mind. The glory of my Redeemer shone upon the vision of my soul without a cloud. He had before seemed to shine upon me with a brightness like the noon-day sun, but now, instead of shining from a particular part of the heavens, He seemed to fill the whole firmament, and to shed His mild and sweet and heavenly and life-giving, joy-inspiring radiance upon me from every point. Above and around me all was light and gladness, and praise to the name of my Redeemer seemed the language of every breath. I cannot but feel that in that state of mind sin had no dominion over me. I feel that God, at that time, gave me the victory through our Lord Jesus Christ.

But I had yet one lesson to learn, and there was probably but one way by which I could learn it; and that by drinking, like Peter, of the cup of sorrow, that I might in future beware. I had been accustomed to say, that if persons believed that they had reason to regard themselves as fully sanctified, there was no necessity for making it known, and the enemy of my soul doubtless knew enough of me, to commence his attack where I was most likely to be overcome.

I was, therefore, led to say within myself, this need not be mentioned, it never shall be said of me that I go about boasting of my own goodness. To boast of my own goodness I certainly felt no disposition, for I clearly saw that all which had been wrought within me was the work of the Holy Spirit, and that of my own I had nothing of which to boast.

But I came to the conclusion not to say, even to my dearest friends, that I had ever thought myself to be cleansed from sin, even for a moment; I would enjoy it alone with God, and let my life bear witness. The consequence was, that when brought where I feared another might suspect me of thinking this of myself, I was led, for the purpose of giving him a better opinion of my humility, to say that I entertained no such opinion.

Herein I fell into sin, by denying what I had believed to have been wrought in me by the Spirit of God. I was now made to feel what I had lost. I had been told that I could not remain in the delightful state in which I had found myself, without confessing to the honor of Christ what I believed He had done for me by His Spirit, but I believed it not. I accordingly made the attempt, and fell into the snare of the wicked one.

I now found the same sins besetting me as before, and bringing me into bondage, and my state precisely what it was, previous to what I believed the Lord had shown me of the blessedness of a pure heart. I knew that by denying that blessed work which the Lord did in me, and by denying it that I might have a reputation for humility with man, I brought leanness and darkness into my own soul.

In this state, however, I was led to desire most earnestly, and to pray most fervently that I might be made like Christ. The burden of my petition was, that I might be made as much like Christ, as it was possible for a soul to become while in the body, and I felt that I could be satisfied with nothing short of this.

After praying thus for a time, I saw most clearly that there was nothing which God was more willing to do, than to make me thus like Christ, and I felt a sweetness of assurance in Him, that it should be granted me.

Now it was that the Lord showed me what must be the consequence of being like Christ, and that I could not possibly have the likeness of Christ without meeting these consequences. I saw that if I would live godly in Christ Jesus, I must suffer persecution, and that I could not be like Christ without being willing to share in His reproach.

The Holy Spirit now showed me the sin which I had committed, in denying what God had done for my soul, and I now saw that while with "**my heart I believeth unto righteousness, with my mouth I must make confession unto salvation**" (Romans 10:10), from being again led into sin. This I had not done. With my heart I had believed unto righteousness, but instead of making confession with my mouth, of the grace which God had shown me, and thereby being saved from the sin of denying it, I had refused to make the confession, and by so doing fell again into the hands of my spiritual foes.

I now saw that, to continue in the enjoyment of that blessing, I must confess the whole and take the consequences. These I knew would not be small. I knew that almost every friend I had on earth would regard me as almost utterly fallen the moment I should make such a confession, and that my brethren in the ministry, whose confidence I had valued above all earthly good, would withdraw their confidence at once, and, in all probability, cast me out from among them.

I had now come truly to the plucking out of the right eye and the cutting off of the right hand—to the point where I must "**forsake father and mother, and brethren and sisters, and wife and children for Christ's sake and the gospel's**" (Matthew 19:29). Could I make the sacrifice? Could I become an outcast from my brethren, and an alien from my mother's children? Could I become as lost, to the friends I had loved most dearly, and have my name cast out as evil, by those whose kind regard I most wished to retain, in order to please my Saviour and enjoy His love, as for a little while He had permitted me to do?

The struggle was severe. It cost me as much to make these sacrifices as it would cost any one of my brethren; but I could not long hesitate. I had prayed that I might continually enjoy the Saviour's love, and He had now shown me what it would cost me—and, blessed be His name, He gave me strength to make the choice of His love, at the sacrifice, if necessary, of every thing that I held dear on earth.

I was enabled to pray, Lord, restore me again to that blessed state of conscious purity and peace, and love to Thee, and blessedness in Thee, which I once enjoyed, and I will confess Thy faithfulness to the world, and let my worthless name be reproached as it may. Save me, Lord, from my sins—redeem me from all iniquity, and give me evidence of it on which I can rely, so that I can go before the world with no hypocritical pretensions to something which I do not possess—let me in deed and in truth be cleansed from all unrighteousness, and have full and satisfactory evidence that Thou hast done this for me, and I will declare Thy faithfulness, and in Thy strength meet all that shall follow.

In this state of mind, I took up the Word of God and came to the following passage, in the words of Paul to the Romans, "**Likewise reckon ye also yourselves to be *dead indeed* unto sin, but alive unto God through Jesus Christ our Lord**" (Romans 6:11).

I had before thought of this passage, and it has seemed to me that there was a meaning in it which I did not understand. I had said in my thoughts, What if I do think myself dead to sin, how will just thinking myself dead to sin, make me thus dead? How will any change be wrought in the state of my heart before God, by my laboring to think so?

Again, I had thought of the injunction, "**Likewise reckon ye also yourselves to be dead indeed unto sin**," and I had said in my heart I will endeavor so to do; but found myself wholly unable to do so in any way that even began to satisfy myself, that I was in truth "**dead to sin**." It was not the comfort of a sincere mistake respecting my own character, that I desired. "**As the hart panteth after the water brooks**," (Psalms 42:1) so panteth my soul after a full conformity to the will of God. I felt that nothing would satisfy me for a moment, but "**to be *dead indeed* unto sin, but alive unto God**" (Romans 6:11).

Nor was it an ambition to have others think me free from sin, that I was seeking to gratify, for if I could have made the whole universe believe me free from sin, while it was not a fact, it would not have begun, in the least degree, to satisfy the longings of my soul. Could I have possessed all the wealth, and received all the honor, and enjoyed all the pleasure, which the whole universe could have lavished upon me, and have been thought by every creature of God in earth and heaven to have been as pure as the Spirits that wait continually before the eternal throne, all this would have done nothing to fill the desires which burned in my heart, to be "**cleansed from all unrighteousness**" (1 John 1:9).

Still, however, with my eye on the injunction, "**Likewise reckon ye also yourselves to be dead indeed unto sin, but alive unto God through Jesus Christ our Lord**" (Romans 6:11), I was not able to see how I should do this, so that it should be *indeed and in truth a reality in the sight of God*; and nothing short of that would satisfy me for a moment.

I now remembered that blessed promise of our divine and glorious and loving Saviour, "**When He, the Spirit of truth, is come, He shall guide you into all truth**" (John 16:13); "**He shall teach you all things, and bring all things to your remembrance, whatsoever I have said unto you**" (John 14:26).

I now cast myself down before the Lord, and prayed in the name of Christ, that the Holy Spirit might guide me into all truth respecting the passage before me, and teach me how to reckon myself dead to sin and alive to God, so that it would be a reality, and not a thing of imagination. Having made known my request, I trusted in Christ that the teachings of the Spirit would be given me, for I knew He had told me, "**Verily, verily I say unto you, whatsoever ye shall ask of the Father in My name, He *will* give it you**" (John 15:16).

I therefore placed my confidence in the Saviour, and believed that, for His sake the Holy Spirit would show me how to "**reckon myself *dead indeed* unto sin; but alive unto God, through Jesus Christ our Lord**" (Romans 6:11). Instantly, while I was even on my knees, with the blessed Bible open before me on those words, there seemed shed upon them a flood of heavenly light, and my very soul filled with unutterable gladness, with "**joy unspeakable and full of glory**" (1 Peter 1:8), with the thought that seemed clear as the brightness of a thousand suns, that I was to reckon myself dead unto sin by trusting my Lord

Jesus Christ to keep me dead to sin, and alive unto God by trusting my Lord Jesus Christ to keep me alive to God.

This I saw would be reckoning myself to be dead indeed unto sin, but alive unto God, through Jesus Christ my Lord. *It was to cease forever from placing my confidence in my own strength, and to rely altogether upon the strength and faithfulness of my blessed Lord Jesus Christ*, to

"Make and keep me
pure within,"

to make and keep me "**dead indeed unto sin**," to make and keep me "**alive unto God**" (Romans 6:11).

And now, if I had found myself that moment monarch of the world, with its crown on my head, its sceptre in my hand, its accumulated treasures at my feet, and every individual among all its multitudes ready to do my bidding, it would not have begun to afford me the joy which I felt, when I saw, as I then did, the privilege which a God of infinite love had granted me, to reckon myself dead indeed unto sin, by trusting my Lord Jesus Christ to make and keep me thus alive.

How glorious and lovely did my Saviour then appear!

"**Or ever I was aware, my soul made me like the chariots of Amminadib**" (Song of Songs 6:12), and if the crown and the sceptre and the riches and the homage of the world had been mine, I should have leaped for joy and run to give Christ the sceptre and the crown, the riches and the homage; and to lay myself in the dust at His feet, to be His humblest, lowliest servant forevermore.

Oh, since I have known my high privilege to reckon myself dead indeed unto sin, but alive unto God, through Jesus Christ my Lord, "**His name has been indeed to me as ointment poured forth**" (Song of Songs 1:3). "**He has kissed me with the kisses of His love, and His love has been better than wine. He has drawn me, and I have run after Him, and the King has brought me into His chambers, and**

made me to be glad and rejoice in Him; therefore will I remember His love more than wine, and (by His strength) I will uprightly love Him" (Song of Songs 1:2, 4).

When the Holy Spirit thus enlightened me respecting the privilege of reckoning myself dead indeed unto sin, but alive unto God through Jesus Christ my Lord, He that moment enabled me to avail myself of the privilege, and I instantly found myself more than restored to that blessed state of conscious purity of heart before God, from which I had fallen, by refusing to confess before men what my Saviour had done for me.

The love of the world was gone, no sinful indulgence had any charm for me. My whole heart was won by Christ, and filled with overflowing love to Him, and I feel that a thousand hearts, had they been mine, would have been most joyfully consecrated to His service. I had no will but His, and no desire of life or death or eternity, but to be disposed of in that way which would secure the highest possible praise to my Redeemer.

I was now delivered from the fear of man, and as I had covenanted with the Lord to confess His faithfulness to the world when He should give me evidence on which I could rely, that I was redeemed from all iniquity, and as I had now found myself, and in a way so glorious and delightful beyond everything I had ever before conceived, made **"*dead* indeed unto sin, but alive unto God through Jesus Christ our Lord,"** and had been so abundantly enlightened respecting the privilege of every Christian to be kept in that state by the faithfulness of the dear Redeemer, I could not for a moment hesitate, that it was my duty to declare to the world, that by the power of the Holy Spirit given me by my own blessed Saviour, I was made **"dead indeed unto sin, but alive unto God through Jesus Christ our Lord"** (Romans 6:11).

Besides, I had once known the bitterness of denying my Saviour here, and the blessed work which He had wrought in me, for the purposes of retaining the good opinion of man; the Holy Spirit had set that sin before me, and I had opened my mouth to the Lord, that if He would restore me, I would bear His reproach. And now He had enabled me once more in His infinite and abounding mercy, "**with the heart to believe unto righteousness,**" and it remained that "**with the mouth I make confession unto salvation**" (Romans 10:10), from falling again into the snare of the devil.

I have been enabled to make this confession to the world—that "**the great God and my Saviour Jesus Christ, who loved me and gave Himself for me, has redeemed me from all iniquity, and purified me unto Himself**" (Titus 2:13-14), that I am "**dead unto sin, and alive unto God through Jesus Christ my Lord**"(Romans 6:11), that "**the God of peace is faithful to sanctify me wholly; and to preserve my whole spirit and soul and body blameless unto the coming of our Lord Jesus Christ**" (1 Thessalonians 5:23), that "**the God of peace, who brought again from the dead our Lord Jesus, that great shepherd of the sheep**" does "**through the blood of the everlasting covenant, make me perfect in every good work to do His will, working in me that which is well pleasing in His sight, through Jesus Christ; to Whom be glory forever and ever. Amen**" (Hebrews 13:20-21).

I felt that in making this confession, I was laying myself and my all, a sacrifice on the altar of my God and Saviour; but that Saviour had led me by His own amazing love, and given me a heart that could deny Him no more, and that was ready and glad at all hazards, to confess His faithfulness and power and love to the world.

I knew that the world would reproach me. I knew that God's professed people would cast out my name as evil. I knew that the friends whom I loved most dearly would many of them, perhaps, weep over me as lost. I knew that the confidence of the churches with which I stood connected, would be withdrawn from me, and perhaps all my past prospects of a maintenance for myself and my household be entirely cut off; but I knew that my Redeemer lived—and that all power was given unto Him in heaven and on earth and that I had only to "**seek first the kingdom of God, and His righteousness**" (Matthew 6:33), nothing doubting that "**He who feeds the fowls of the air, and clothes the lilies of the field, as Solomon was never arrayed in all his glory**" (Matthew 6:26,28-29), would surely feed and clothe me and mine.

In this state of mind I did, at the altar of my God, make confession of what God had taught me of His truth, and of what I had been made to feel of His purifying, sanctifying grace in Jesus Christ; and thus I discharged a duty, to which I am sure I never could have been led by anything, but a once-crucified and now glorified Saviour's love, manifested to me by the Holy Ghost. I have no more doubt that I was constrained to this step by the love of Christ, than I have that Christ or my own soul has a being. I know I was not led to it by a love of the world, for I never could have done it, until the last vestige of the love of the world had taken from me. I know that until I had made of the whole world an entire sacrifice to Christ, I never could have thus held myself up to scorn.

On the morning of the day which immediately followed the Sabbath when I first "witnessed this confession" before men, I had a season of communion with God, of which I will speak, because I think it may do good. I was alone in my chamber, and meditating upon some passages of Scripture, which made mention of the faithfulness of God. Such as the following: "**God is *faithful*, by whom ye were called unto the fellowship of His Son Jesus Christ**" (1 Corinthians 1:9). "***Faithful* is He that hath called you, to sanctify you wholly; and to preserve your whole spirit and soul and body blameless unto the coming of our Lord Jesus Christ**" (1 Thessalonians 5:24, 23). "**God is *faithful*, who will not suffer you to be tempted above that ye are able; but will with the temptation also make way for your escape, that ye may be able to bear it**" (1 Corinthians 10.13). "**And I saw heaven opened, and** behold a white horse; and He that sat upon him was called *Faithful and True*" (Revelation 19:11). "**His name is also called the Word of God. And He hath on His vesture and on His thigh a name written, KING OF KINGS, AND LORD OF LORDS**" (Revelation 19:13,16).

While reflecting thus upon the faithfulness of my God and Saviour, my whole soul seemed heaved with inexpressible emotions, and poured out in floods of gushing love at my Redeemer's feet. I felt that I had forsaken all for Him, and could now only leave myself in His hands, and commit all my interests to His disposal. And now in view of the safety of trusting my all with Him, my soul exulted with amazing gladness, and I could only walk my room weeping aloud for joy, and pouring out my tears of overflowing delight, as I uttered again and again the single expression, "my faithful God, my faithful God!"

Since that time, I have had various conflicts with Satan, but I have never for a moment doubted the faithfulness of my Redeemer in saving all His people from their sins, who will believe on His name for that blessing; and I see most clearly, that the only reason why any Christian is not saved from sin, is "**because of unbelief**" (Romans 11:20).

I have by no means been all that I hope, or expect to be; for I see that it is the privilege of the Christian that has been redeemed from all iniquity, still to "**forget the things which are behind, and reach forth unto those things which are before**" (Philippians 3:13), and "**beholding as in a glass the glory of the Lord, to be changed into the same image from glory to glory, even as by the Spirit of the Lord**" (2 Corinthians 3:18).

I believe that to be cleansed from all unrighteousness is by no means the height of the Christian's privilege on earth; that beyond that he may go on "**to comprehend with all saints what is the breadth, and length, and depth, and height, and to know the love of Christ, which passeth knowledge,**" and to be filled more and more "**with all the fullness of God**" (Ephesians 3:18, 19). And that even then, we may still say to Him with the apostle—"**Now unto Him that is able to do exceeding abundantly above all that we ask or think, according to the power that worketh in us, unto Him be glory by Christ Jesus throughout all ages, world without end. Amen**" (Ephesians 3:20-21).

You have now seen, brethren, in what I have related to you of the leadings and teachings of God's Spirit with my own soul, why I cannot regard your admonition, and desist from preaching the doctrine of entire sanctification by faith in Christ. I could not do it, without regarding myself as a traitor to my blessed Lord and Master, Who has made to me—a miserable, unworthy, hell-deserving worm of the dust—manifestations of His presence and love, bright and glorious, far beyond anything which I once could have conceived. I believe "**He is faithful to sanctify His people wholly, and to preserve their whole spirit and soul and body blameless unto His coming**" (1 Thessalonians 5:24, 23). I feel that "**necessity is laid upon me; yea, woe is unto me, if I preach not this gospel**" (1 Corinthians 9:16). Like Jonah fleeing to Tarshish, I once attempted to escape the discharge of the duty. Like Jeremiah, "**I said, I will not make mention of Him, nor speak any more in His name. But His word was in mine heart as a burning fire shut up in my bones, and I was weary with forbearing, and I could not stay**" (Jeremiah 20:9).

Once I denied the faithfulness of my Redeemer; but He forgave me, and has restored me to the enjoyment of His love, and has, as I firmly believe, in faithfulness to His own promise, "**circumcised my heart to love Him with all my heart, and with all my soul**" (Deuteronomy 30:6). I must speak it to the world. Let Him have the glory, and let me bear the reproach which I must bear for His sake.

I must confess it to the world, for the purpose of making known, as far as I am able, with His blessing, to all God's people, their high privileges in Christ Jesus. For "**I certify you, brethren, that this gospel** which is preached of me is not after man. For I neither received it of man, neither was I taught it, but by the revelation of Jesus Christ" (Galatians 1:11-12). And now "Whether it be right in the sight of God to hearken unto you more than unto God, judge ye. For I cannot but speak the things which I have seen and heard" (Acts 4:19-20).

REASON TWO

2. I cannot desist from preaching the doctrine of sanctification, and from testifying to my own experience of it, for the very same reasons that you cannot desist from preaching the doctrine of regeneration, and testifying to your own experience of that. Suppose that you were to insist that "Except a man be born again, he cannot see the kingdom of God" (John 3:3), but when asked whether you or any one else had enjoyed that blessing, should say, "By no means. It is an important and dangerous error for any man to think so; it never takes place until death." How much influence would such preaching exert? How many would be born again through such instrumentality?

You feel yourselves under necessity, therefore, on that subject, to maintain that regeneration is a matter of experience, and that you and many others do enjoy it. But while you tell your people that they ought to be free from sin, and are wholly inexcusable for not being so, and while you pray that they may be redeemed from all iniquity, they know perfectly well that you have no expectation that it will take place while they live, and hence all your exhortations and prayers are wholly lost. Your people know that you expect that they will live along in sin until death, and that while you exhort them to be free from sin, you show them no way by which they may become so, and maintain that it would be an important and dangerous error for them to expect to be so until they die. Hence, all your efforts for the sanctification of God's professing people, are rendered perfectly nugatory.

For myself, therefore, I feel bound to tell professing Christians that there is a way whereby they may "**cleanse themselves from all filthiness of the flesh and spirit, and perfect holiness in the fear of God**" (2 Corinthians 7:1), that it may be done through the promises of God, which "**are all yea, and Amen in Jesus Christ**" (2 Corinthians 1:20).

When, therefore, with the apostle, "**I labour, striving according to God's Spirit, which worketh in me mightily, by warning every man, and teaching every man in all wisdom to present every man perfect in Christ Jesus**" (Colossians 1:29, 28), I feel that I am not urging them to chase a phantom, which, however earnestly and laboriously sought, will elude their grasp till death; but that I am leading them to the enjoyment of a blessed and glorious reality, which is treasured up for them in Christ, and which they may every one of them secure and most richly enjoy.

And when I am permitted, through the exceeding riches of God's love in Christ Jesus, to say that I have experienced of the grace which I present to their acceptance, I have left them stripped of all excuses and palliations for their sins, and may therefore hope that God's Spirit will attend His truth, and lead them in the way of knowledge and under-standing. I can say to Christians, "**This is the will of God, even your sanctification**" (1 Thessalonians 4:3). "**God hath not called us unto uncleanness, but unto holiness**" (1 Thessalonians 4:7), while you by your own principles are obliged to tell them, that they are shut up, in some measure at least, to a life of sin. Brethren, I cannot stand on such ground, and therefore I must disregard your admonition.

There seems to me to be a wonderful and strange inconsistency, in urging Christians to holiness of heart and life, and at the same time telling them that they never can be without sin while they live, and that if they think that Christ, who was manifested to take away their sins, will ever do it till He takes away their breath, they have embraced important and dangerous error. I feel constrained to say, in faithfulness to Christ and His dear people, though some may think it unkind, that those who attempt to maintain such ground, seem to me to be, and in a very important sense "**shutting up of the kingdom of heaven against men: neither entering themselves, nor suffering those who would enter to go in**" (Matthew 23:13).

When the watchmen of Israel cry out in the ears of the people, that no man ever did or will abide in Christ and sin not, on earth, that God who has sworn to do it, and raised up Christ our horn of salvation to perform the oath, never will "**grant unto us, that we being delivered out of the hand of our enemies might serve Him without fear, in holiness and righteousness before Him, all the days of our life**" (Luke 1:74-75), what can we expect, but that many who desire deliverance from sin, will despair of attaining it, and submit in despondency to the will of their spiritual foes, and groan away their lives in grievous bondage, when they might be enjoying the liberty wherewith Christ would make them free; and that others, glad to have such an excuse for their sins, will comfort themselves in their worldliness, and their unhallowed indulgences by the feeling that they are not expected, while they live, to be free from sin.

I will not attempt to conceal it, that this looks to me like a subtle and dangerous snare of the great enemy of Christ and His church. Herein it seems to me lies the "important and dangerous error," and not in telling Christians that their Redeemer "**is faithful to sanctify them wholly, and to preserve their whole spirit and soul and body blameless to H is coming**" (1 Thessalonians 5:23), when they will believe in Him for that blessing.

REASON THREE

3. I cannot regard your admonition because those Scriptures on which you rely as testimony that no Christian ever does so "**abide in Christ as to sin not**," seem to me to have no bearing that way.

Take, for example, the single passage quoted in the report of your committee, and adopted by you as ample proof of the correctness of your views.

"**There is not a just man upon earth, that doeth good, and sinneth not**" (Ecclesiastes 7:20). Let us apply this to the experience of Paul. "**I have fought a good fight, I have finished my course, I have kept the faith**" (2 Timothy 4:7). What arrogant, presumptuous language has Paul here used! He must have been puffed up with spiritual pride! Did he not know that the Bible expressly declares "**There is not a just man upon earth, that doeth good, and sinneth not?**" How dare he say, "**I have fought a good fight?**"

But suppose Paul were allowed to step forth in his own defense, and taking the ground ascribed to him by those who regard the doctrine of entire sanctification by a faith in Christ as "an important and dangerous error," should begin to say, "I acknowledge that there is much sin in my heart, and that my best actions are defiled with it, but still I think I have had some love of God, some desire to glorify Him by doing His will, some readiness to spend and be spent in His service, and that I have in some things sincerely labored for the advancement of His cause." We may come forward still and say, Paul, you are certainly mistaken; you think of yourself more highly than you ought to think; for it is a positive undeniable declaration of God's own Word that "**There is not a just man upon earth, that doeth good, and sinneth not,**" and, therefore, Paul, your assumption that there is any good thing in you is forever silenced.

Your text, therefore, brethren, stands just as entirely and fully opposed to your views of truth as to mine; and in my apprehension has nothing to do either with the one or the other. The truth is this. There is a large class of Scripture texts which are designed to set forth the truth, that by nature and by practice until regeneration, all mankind are "**evil,** only evil, and that continually" (Genesis 6:5). But "**if any man be in Christ, he is a new creature: old things are passed away; behold, and all things have become new**" (2 Corinthians 5:17). The character of such a one is precisely what it was not before; and those passages of Scripture which described his character before, cannot describe it now.

Consequently we find that the Scriptures used to describe the two characters, stand in direct opposition to each other. Accordingly, while it is said that "**There is not a just man upon earth, that doeth good, and sinneth not**" (Ecclesiastes 7:20), it is also said, that those who "**were sometime alienated and enemies in their minds by wicked works**" (Colossians 1:21)—shall be presented "**holy and unblameable and unreproveable in His sight, if they continue in the faith, grounded and settled, and be not moved away from the hope of the gospel**" (Colossians 1:22-23), that in fulfillment of the oath of God through Christ, their horn of salvation, it shall be "**granted them, that they being delivered out of the hand of their enemies might serve Him without fear, in holiness and righteousness before Him, all the days of their lives**" (Luke 1:74-75); that those who "**abide in Christ sin not**" (1 John 3:6), and that "**He who hath called them is faithful to sanctify them wholly, and to preserve them wholly, and to preserve their whole spirit, and soul and body, blameless, unto the coming of Christ**" (1 Thessalonians 5:23).

"**All the promises of God pledging their sanctification, are yea, and Amen in Christ, unto the glory of God by them**" (2 Corinthians 1:20), and when they believe in Christ for the fulfillment of these promises they cannot fail. Most clearly therefore, to my mind, these passages of Scripture which are relied on to prove that God's people never will be "**presented perfect in Christ Jesus**" (Colossians 1:28), while they live, are designed to set forth the characters of the unrenewed, and not the characters of such as are "**in Christ Jesus**" (Romans 6:1), and who are therefore "**NEW CREATURES, OLD THINGS HAVING PASSED

AWAY, AND ALL THINGS BECOME NEW" (2 Corinthians 5:17). In the nature of the case, what is true of the one class, cannot be true of the other, for they are designedly set forth in the Bible as perfect opposites.

But again. Suppose we admit, that among the saints of the Old Testament not a man lived without sin; although it was said of Isaiah, after he had made confession of his uncleanness, and his lips had been touched with a live coal from the altar of God, "**Lo, this hath touched thy lips; and thine iniquity is taken away, and thy sin purged**" (Isaiah 6:7). But admit that the Old Testament saints were at all times defiled with the guilt of actual transgressions, is there no privilege granted to God's people now, that was not afforded to the early saints?

"**Whom having not seen, ye love; in whom, though now ye see him not, yet believing, ye rejoice with joy unspeakable and full of glory:** *receiving the end of your faith, even the salvation of your souls.* **Of which salvation the prophets have inquired and searched diligently,** *who prophesied of the grace that should come unto you.* **Searching what, or what manner of time the Spirit of Christ which was in them did signify, when it testified beforehand the sufferings of Christ,** *and the glory that should follow.* **Unto whom it was revealed,** *that not unto themselves, but unto us they did minister the things, which are now reported* **unto you by them that have preached the gospel unto you with the Holy Ghost sent down from heaven; which things the angels desire to look into**" (1 Peter 1:8-12).

What is this end of faith, even the salvation of the soul? Of which salvation the prophets inquired and searched diligently? What is this grace of which they prophesied, coming unto the saints scattered abroad, to whom Peter wrote? What was the glory that was to follow the sufferings of Christ? What were the things which the prophets ministered, not unto themselves, but to those to whom the gospel was afterwards preached by the Holy Ghost sent down from heaven?

What did Christ mean when He said, "**This is My blood of** *the New Testament*" (Matthew 26:28)? What did Paul mean by that new and better covenant of which Christ was the mediator and surety? And what did Christ mean when He said, "**He that is least in the kingdom of heaven is greater than John the Baptist, than whom there had never been, up to his day, a greater prophet**" (Luke 7:28)? And what did Zacharias mean, when he said, "**Blessed be the Lord God of Israel; for** *He hath visited and redeemed His people*, **and hath raised up an horn of salvation, to perform the mercy promised unto the fathers, the covenant, the oath which He sware**" (Luke 1:68, 69, 72, 73)? What is all this but the blessing of the new covenant spoken of by Jeremiah, and repeatedly spoken of by Paul to the Hebrews:

"**I** *will*, **(since they brake My old covenant), make a new covenant**," "**I** *will* **put My laws into their hearts and in their minds will I write them**" (Hebrews 10:16), "**I will** (and with an oath the mighty God hath said it) **grant unto you that ye being delivered out of the hand of your enemies may serve Me without fear, in holiness and righteousness before me all the days of your life**" (Luke 1:73-75). This, then, is the peculiar covenant privilege of New Testament saints—SALVATION FROM THEIR SINS.

This explains all the Scriptures which I have quoted, and therefore whatever might have been true of Old Testament saints, it is now the peculiar privilege of God's people to be redeemed from all iniquity, and for this they have only to believe in the Mediator of this new covenant, for this is God's covenant with them, when He shall take away their sins. It is, therefore, the privilege of the new covenant that I am to hold up before the people of God, and urge to the full enjoyment of it; and thus seek, like the apostles, to obtain "**sufficiency of God to be an** *able minister of the New Testament*, **not of the letter that killeth, but the spirit that giveth life**" (2 Corinthians 3:6).

Your application of Old Testament declarations of the universal sinfulness of men, therefore, to show the privileges of New Testament believers, is, in my view, a great mistake, and shows you to be still ministers of the Old Testament, instead of being, as you should be, "able ministers of the New Testament." For this reason, then, I cannot heed your admonition. I wish to be a minister of the New Testament, not of the Old.

REASON FOUR

4. I will now state one more reason, why I cannot give heed to your admonition, and then I shall have done.

There is a dying bed a little before me, and a judgment seat where I expect to stand and give account for all the actions of my life.

Can I tell the people of God that they have no Saviour from sin during their whole lives; that live long as they may, and labor as hard as they may to find out the path of life, and pray as fervently as they may, and trust in their Saviour for the fulfillment of the promises as fully as they may, they are doomed hopelessly to sin against the Redeemer they love, more or less, even to their dying hour; that all their cries and struggles for help are vain, and that they must be, to some extent, rebels against the heart of infinite love, until the grim monster death appears for their deliverance? To me it looks like casting dust in the eyes of such as wish to see a way whereby they may be enabled to love their God and Saviour with a perfect heart; and "**sewing pillows to the armholes**" (Ezekiel 13:18) of those who wish to pass comfortably through life in their remaining corruptions, hoping to find a Saviour from sin, only when all opportunity for sinful enjoyment has passed away.

I feel, brethren, that I could not go in peace to my dying pillow, or appear at the great tribunal, expecting the approbation of My Judge, if I did not tell God's people that He has promised to "**circumcise their heart, and the heart of their seed, to love the LORD their God with** all their heart, and with all their soul" (Deuteronomy 30:6); to "**sprinkle clean water upon them, and make them clean: from all their filthiness, and from all their idols, to cleanse them**" (Ezekiel 36:25), and that these, with many other exceeding great and precious promises, were given for the express purpose, that through them, they might "**cleanse themselves from all filthiness of the flesh and spirit, perfect holiness in the fear of God**" (2 Corinthians 7:1)—that by these promises, they might become "**partakers of the divine nature, having escaped the corruption that is in the world through lust**" (2 Peter 1:4).

I feel it to be a matter of unspeakable importance to the honor of Christ and the good of His cause, and the holiness and peace of His suffering heritage, that they be made to know that there has "**come out of Zion a Deliverer to turn away ungodliness from Jacob**" (Romans 11:26), and that God has said, respecting this Deliverer, "**This is My covenant with them when I shall take away their sins**" (Romans 11:27). It seems to me that God's professing people do not know their Deliverer, and there are vast multitudes who seem altogether unwilling to know Him. Hence the reproach cast upon such as declare that there is a "**Deliverer to turn away ungodliness from them and take away their sins**" (Romans 11:26-27). But I see not how I can lie down in peace on my dying pillow, or meet the Saviour in judgment before the universe, unless I do what in me lies to make Him known. I feel constrained to cry in the ears of the church, Behold your Deliverer; He has come to turn away ungodliness from you, and to take away your sins. Look to Him; believe on His name, and let "**your iniquity be taken away, and your sins be purged**" (Isaiah 6:7).

And now, brethren, I have done. I cannot, for the reasons I have named, and in view of my final account; I dare not listen to your admonition for a moment. With my name you must do what you think right before God, and in view of an approaching judgment. I have no further defense to make. If you cannot own me as one of your number while I tell the church of Christ that He was manifested to take away their sins, and that they may and ought so to abide in Him that they sin not—that it is my privilege and theirs so to abide in Christ, that it is my belief that through the grace of God I do so abide in Him; if such a confidence in my Redeemer for the fulfillment of God's exceeding great and precious promises, must still make me, in your estimation, an advocate of important and dangerous error, then just blot me out of your book, and let the transaction be recorded, as it will be, in the book of God, to be reviewed before the universe in the final day. That I hold the doctrine which you call important and dangerous error, and believe it to be the brightest glory of my bleeding Saviour's gospel, is true; and I know that, if you knew the blessedness of trusting fully in Christ as your Redeemer from all iniquity, there is not a man of you, who would not choose that his tongue should perish, rather than be used to pronounce such a doctrine importantly and dangerously erroneous. But if you still adhere to that opinion, I must consider myself as no longer of your number, and you must do to me and with me as you think our Lord and Master requires. "**Now may the God of peace, that brought again from the dead our Lord Jesus, that great Shepherd of the sheep, through the blood of the everlasting covenant, make you perfect in every good work to do His will, working in you that which is wellpleasing in His sight, through Jesus Christ; to whom be glory forever and ever. Amen**" (Hebrews 13:20-21).

Yours in the gospel,
CHARLES FITCH

"Come Out of Her, My People."

by Charles Fitch,
From *Second Advent of Christ*, July, 1843.

Revelation 18:1-5: "**And after these things I saw another angel come down from heaven, having great power; and the earth was lightened with his glory.**

"**And he cried mightily with a strong voice, saying, Babylon the great is fallen, is fallen, and is become the habitation of devils, and the hold of every foul spirit, and a cage of every unclean and hateful bird. For all nations have drunk of the wine of the wrath of her fornication, and the kings of the earth have committed fornication with her, and the merchants of the earth are waxed rich through the abundance of her delicacies.**

"**And I heard another voice from heaven, saying, Come out of her, my people, that ye be not partakers of her sins, and that ye receive not of her plagues. For her sins have reached unto heaven, and God hath remembered her iniquities.**"

Revelation 18:21: "**And a mighty angel took up a stone like a great millstone, and cast it into the sea, saying, Thus with violence shall that great city Babylon be thrown down, and shall be found no more at all.**"

Revelation 14:6-20: "**And I saw another angel fly in the midst of heaven, having the everlasting gospel to preach unto them that dwell on the earth, and to every nation, and kindred, and tongue, and people,**

"**Saying with a loud voice, Fear God, and give glory to him; for the hour of his judgment is come: and worship him that made heaven, and earth, and the sea, and the fountains of waters.**

"And there followed another angel, saying, Babylon is fallen, is fallen, that great city, because she made all nations drink of the wine of the wrath of her fornication.

"And the third angel followed them, saying with a loud voice, If any man worship the beast and his image, and receive his mark in his forehead, or in his hand, the same shall drink of the wine of the wrath of God, which is poured out without mixture into the cup of his indignation; and he shall be tormented with fire and brimstone in the presence of the holy angels, and in the presence of the Lamb: and the smoke of their torment ascendeth up for ever and ever: and they have no rest day nor night, who worship the beast and his image, and whosoever receiveth the mark of his name. "Here is the patience of the saints: here are they that keep the commandments of God, and the faith of Jesus.

"And I heard a voice from heaven saying unto me, Write, Blessed are the dead which die in the Lord from henceforth: Yea, saith the Spirit, that they may rest from their labours; and their works do follow them.

"And I looked, and behold a white cloud, and upon the cloud one sat like unto the Son of man, having on his head a golden crown, and in his hand a sharp sickle. And another angel came out of the temple, crying with a loud voice to him that sat on the cloud, Thrust in thy sickle, and reap: for the time is come for thee to reap; for the harvest of the earth is ripe. And he that sat on the cloud thrust in his sickle on the earth; and the earth was reaped.

"And another angel came out of the temple which is in heaven, he also having a sharp sickle. And another angel came out from the altar, which had power over fire; and cried with a loud cry to him that had the sharp sickle, saying, Thrust in thy sharp sickle, and gather the clusters of the vine of the earth; for her grapes are fully ripe. And the angel thrust in his sickle into the earth, and gathered the vine of the earth, and cast it into the great winepress of the wrath of God. And the winepress was trodden without the city, and blood came out of the winepress, even unto the horse bridles, by the space of a thousand and six hundred furlongs."

1. 1. What is Babylon?
2. 2. What is the fall of Babylon?
3. 3. What is it for God's people to come out of Babylon?
4. 4. What will be the consequences for refusing to do it?

1. What is Babylon?

It is Antichrist: all those to whom Christ will say at His appearing, "**Those Mine enemies, who would not that I should reign over them, bring hither, and slay them before Me.**" (Luke 19:27). It is everything belonging to the wine of the earth, which, at the appearance of the one like the Son of man on a white cloud, is to be reaped, and cast into the great wine press of the wrath of God.

What is Antichrist? "**Beloved, believe not every spirit, but try the spirits whether they are of God: because many false prophets are gone out into the world. Hereby know ye the Spirit of God: Every spirit that confesseth that Jesus Christ is come in the flesh is of God: And every spirit that confesseth not that Jesus Christ is come in the flesh is not of God: AND THIS IS THAT SPIRIT OF ANTICHRIST, whereof ye have heard that it should come; and even now already is it in the world**" (1 John 4:1-3). "**For many deceivers are entered into the world, WHO CONFESS NOT THAT JESUS CHRIST IS COME IN THE FLESH. THIS IS A DECEIVER AND AN ANTICHRIST**" (2 John 1:7).

It must be admitted that a spirit which is of God, while it confesses that Jesus Christ is come in the flesh, will readily assent and conform to all the objects for which He came. To confess with the lips that Jesus Christ is come in the flesh, and yet to be opposed in heart and life to the objects for which He came, is certainly to be Antichrist. The spirit therefore which is of God, while it confesses that Jesus Christ is come in the flesh, will cordially embrace, and heartily enter into all the objects for which He was thus manifested; all else must be Antichrist.

What, then, was the end for which Jesus Christ was manifested in the flesh? **"Then opened He their understanding, that they might understand the Scriptures, and said unto them, Thus it is written, and thus it behooved Christ to suffer, and to rise from the dead the third day: And that repentance and remission of sins should be preached in his name among all nations, beginning at Jerusalem"** (Luke 24:45-47). This was one object of Christ's coming in the flesh; and when Peter rebuked Him for foretelling such things concerning Himself, Christ turned and rebuked Peter, saying **"Get thee behind me, Satan: for thou savourest not the things that be of God, but the things that be of men"** (Mark 8:33). Peter then was at that time Antichrist, in being opposed to the suffering of Christ in the flesh.

But did Jesus Christ come in the flesh for no purpose but to suffer? Hear Peter on the day of Pentecost, after he had been baptized with the Holy Ghost, and fully qualified to set forth the objects of Christ's coming. **"Men and brethren, let me freely speak unto you of the patriarch David, that he is both dead and buried, and his sepulchre is with us unto this day. Therefore being a prophet, and knowing that GOD HAD SWORN WITH AN OATH TO HIM, THAT OF THE FRUIT OF HIS LOINS, ACCORDING TO THE FLESH, HE WOULD RAISE UP CHRIST TO SIT ON HIS THRONE; He seeing this before spake of the resurrection of Christ"** Acts 2:29-31. Here

73

we are informed that God had sworn with an oath to David, that He would raise up Christ in the flesh to reign on David's throne, and was raised up from the dead with flesh and bones for that purpose, and in that same body ascended to heaven, and angels declared that He would so come again, in like manner as He went into Heaven. Now, as His ascension is personal, His coming must be personal.

Isaiah had prophesied, in his 9th chapter, "**Unto us a child is born, unto us a Son is given: and the government shall be upon His shoulder: and His name shall be called Wonderful, Counsellor, The mighty God, The everlasting Father, The Prince of Peace. Of the increase of His government and peace there shall be no end, UPON THE THRONE OF DAVID, AND UPON HIS KINGDOM, to order it, and to establish it with judgment and with justice from henceforth even forever. The zeal of the LORD of hosts will perform this**" (Isaiah 9:6-7).

Again, Jeremiah 33:15-17: "**In those days, and at that time, will I cause the Branch of righteousness to grow up unto David; and He shall execute judgment and righteousness in the land. In those days shall Judah be saved, and Jerusalem shall dwell safely: and this is the name wherewith she shall be called, The LORD our righteousness. For thus saith the LORD; David shall never want A MAN TO SIT UPON THE THRONE of the house of Israel.**" And verses 20-21: "**Thus saith the LORD; If ye can break My covenant of the day, and My covenant of the night, and that there should not be day and night in their season; then may also My covenant be broken with David My servant, that he should not have a son to reign upon his throne.**"

"**And the angel said unto her, Fear not, Mary: for thou hast found favour with God. And, behold, thou shalt conceive in thy womb, and bring forth a Son, and shalt call His name JESUS. He shall be great, and shall be called the Son of the Highest: and the Lord God shall give unto Him the throne of His father David: and**

74

He shall reign over the house of Jacob forever; and of His kingdom there shall be no end" (Luke 1:30-33).

Now as surely as the birth of Christ was personal, and not spiritual, His life, His death, His resurrection, His ascension, personal, so surely His coming must be. As He has taught, in the 19th of Luke, He is now gone into a far country to receive to Himself a kingdom and to return; and "**He shall so come again in like manner as ye have seen Him go into heaven**" (Acts 1:11). In the 89th Psalm we read, "**Once have I sworn by My holiness that I will not lie unto David. His seed shall endure forever, and his throne as the sun before Me. It shall be established forever as the moon, and as a faithful witness in heaven**" (Psalms 89:35-37).

Then Jesus Christ has come in the flesh to sit on David's throne; He is to sit upon it personally and forever. For at the sounding of the seventh trumpet, there shall be heard great voices in heaven saying, "**THE KINGDOMS OF THIS WORLD are become the kingdoms of our Lord, and of His Christ; and HE SHALL REIGN FOREVER AND EVER**" (Revelation 11:15). "**He shall have dominion also from sea to sea, and from the river unto the ends of the earth.**" (Psalms 72:8). He said indeed at the bar of Pilate, "**My kingdom is not of this world**" (John 18:36); and for the reason that the earth which now is, is kept in store, reserved unto fire against the day of judgment and perdition of ungodly men; and as Christ's kingdom can have no end, God has promised a new earth wherein dwelleth righteousness, and has said, "**As the new heavens and the new earth, which I will make, shall remain before me, saith the LORD, so shall your seed and your name remain**" (Isaiah 66:22. See the 65th and 66th chapters of Isaiah and the 3rd chapter of 2 Peter).

In the new earth wherein dwelleth righteousness, therefore, Christ will sit personally and eternally on David's throne, ruling the world in righteousness, and of His kingdom "**There shall be no end**" (Luke 1:33). Thus, as Paul said to the Hebrews, Christ "**for the joy that was**

75

set before Him endured the cross, despising the shame, and is set down at the right hand of the throne of God" (Hebrews 12:2). He also tells us that Christ is "from henceforth expecting until His enemies shall be made His footstool" (Hebrews 10:13). The joy set before Him, and for which He endured His sufferings on the cross, must be the joy of His eternal kingdom, when He shall reign in glory and blessedness with all His saints. Christ then was manifested in the flesh, and was raised up, and is now immortalized, for the express purpose of coming again, in like manner as He went up into heaven, to reign eternally over the entire world, on David's throne. Hence it follows that whoever is opposed to the PERSONAL REIGN of Jesus Christ over this world on David's throne, is ANTICHRIST; for though he may admit that Jesus Christ is come in the flesh, he is opposed to the object for which He came, and therefore must be Antichrist; for "the kingdoms of this world must become the kingdoms of our Lord, and of His Christ; and He shall reign forever and ever" (Revelation 11:15).

We have therefore only to inquire who is OPPOSED TO THE PERSONAL REIGN OF CHRIS T ON DAVID'S THRONE, in order to ascertain who is ANTICHRIST, or who is IN BABYLON, to be destroyed when Christ shall appear in the clouds of heaven to establish His kingdom.

Who, then, is opposed to the personal reign of Christ on David's throne?

First: The entire Roman Catholic Church. The primitive church believed in the personal reign of Christ, and looked and longed for it, and waited for His appearing, and loved it as the apostles has done before them. Justin Martyr, one of the primitive Christians, declares that this was the faith in which all the orthodox in the primitive church agreed. But when the papacy came into power, they concluded to have Christ reign, not personally, but spiritually, and hence the pope entered into the stead of Christ, and undertook to rule the world for Him, claiming to be God's vicegerent on earth.

Inasmuch therefore as the papists wish to retain their power, we find them all opposed to the idea of Christ's coming to establish a personal reign. They are willing that Christ should reign spiritually, provided they can be His acknowledged agents, and thus bring the world to bow down wholly to their dictation, and use God's authority for their own aggrandizement. But to the idea of Christ's coming to establish personal reign, they are decidedly and bitterly hostile. They will not confess that Jesus Christ has come in the flesh to reign. They are willing to admit that He has come to suffer, but they will not award Him His crown, and consent to His taking His seat on the throne of David, while they bow down and worship. Hence they are Antichrist. When the Israelites of old departed from the true God and worshipped idols and made these their dependence, God charged them with the sin of whoredom toward Himself. The Catholics, while claiming to be the church of God, have always, when they could, looked for support of the secular power, instead of trusting God to maintain them. Hence God accuses them of "**committing fornication with the kings of the earth**" (Revelation 17:2); and the Romish church is called "**the great whore**" (Revelation 17:1) that did corrupt the nations; drawing them from the worship and service of the true God, to support her in her nameless and horrid abominations. But,

Second: Is the Catholic Church only, opposed to the personal reign of Christ? What shall we say of Protestant Christendom in this respect? Among all the denominations into which the Protestant Church is divided, where is one that is not decidedly hostile to the Bible truth that Christ has been raised up to sit personally on David's throne? Indeed, where has such a notion originated, as that Christ is to have only a spiritual reign? There is nothing in the Bible that furnishes the least shadow of a foundation for such an idea. Paul has, however, given us a clue to the origin of the very thing: "**For the time will come when they will not endure sound doctrine; but after their own lusts shall they heap to themselves teachers, having itching ears; and they shall turn away their ears from the truth, and shall be turned unto fables**" (2 Timothy 4:3-4).

This is, at present, true of all denominations of Protestant Christendom. The sound, Scriptural doctrine of the personal reign of Christ on David's throne cannot now be endured, and hence the teachers which the various sects have been heaping to themselves have turned away their ears to the groundless fable of a spiritual reign of Christ, during what is called a temporal millennium, when they expect all the world to be converted; and each sect is expecting at that time to have the predominant influence. Each one of these sects is willing to rule the world as the Papists have done FOR Christ, but no one of them is willing to have Christ come in person to rule the world for Himself, while they take their place at His feet to do His bidding, nor are they willing to listen for a moment to what the Bible says respecting Christ's personal coming. It is only here and there, among all the sects, that a place of worship can be obtained for the purpose of showing the people what is contained in the Bible respecting Christ's coming and kingdom. Nor are these sects honest in their pretended attachment even to the spiritual reign of Christ, for there is not a sect among them all that will now allow Christ to reign over them in a spiritual sense, inasmuch as they do not as a sect make Christ's principles and precepts their rules of life. No one sect can be found, that live by Christ's rules. They would call it ultraism to think of doing so. Besides, if they had been sincere in their desires for the spiritual reign of Christ, they might have sent the gospel into every dwelling on the face of the earth long ago. Christ said, By their fruits ye shall know them, and the fruit which He expected His true disciples to bear was obedience to His precepts. **"If ye love me, keep my commandments"** (John 14:15).

His precepts were such as these: **"Lay not up for yourselves treasures upon earth, where moth and rust doth corrupt, and where thieves break through and steal"** (Matthew 6:19). **"Sell that ye have, and give alms"** (Luke 12:33). **"Give to him that asketh thee, and from him that would borrow of thee turn not thou away"** (Matthew 5:42). Be merciful and do good, **"and lend, hoping for nothing again"** (Luke 6:35). **"Bless them which persecute you"** (Romans 12:14). **"Do good to them that hate you, and pray for them which despitefully use you, and persecute you"** (Matthew 5:44).

"By such fruits were they to be known" (Matthew 7:16). The practical motto in this day is, BY THEIR CREEDS YE SHALL KNOW THEM. If a man subscribes to an orthodox creed, and covenants to deny Himself all ungodliness and every worldly lust, he may after serve the devil with both hands, and yet be regarded as a good Christian. With a Presbyterian, or an Episcopalian, or a Methodist, or a Baptist Book of Discipline in his pocket, he may gird up all the energies of his being to amass wealth, and live solely for purposes of personal aggrandizement, and yet pass among professedly Christian sects as a disciple, a follower of Him who on earth had not where to lay His head, and who has said to His followers, Lay not up for yourselves treasures on earth. Though the Bible says, **"They that will be rich fall into temptation and a snare, and into many foolish and hurtful lusts, which drown men in destruction and perdition"** (1 Timothy 6:9).

The various sects of Christendom expect that their members will make the accumulation of wealth the object of their lives. And yet they profess to be desiring the spiritual reign of Christ, and to be living for the conversion of the world to the religion of the crucified Nazarene. Tell them, however, that Christ is coming in person, according to the oath of God, to carry out the principles of His own religion forever, and they are ready to fight against it with all their might.

We are living the very state of things predicted by our Saviour, **"And because iniquity shall abound, the love of many shall wax cold"** (Matthew 24:12). To such an extent has the love of this world abounded in the hearts of those who say they are Christ's that nothing is so unwelcome to the mass of them as to tell them that their Saviour, whom they profess to regard as their best friend, is soon coming to take His people to be with Him.

The apostle John writes as follows: **"Love not the world, neither the things that are in the world. If any man love the world, the love of the Father is not in him. For all that is in the world, the lust of the flesh, and the lust of the eyes, and the pride of life, is not of the Father, but is of the world. And the world passeth away, and the lust thereof: but he that DOETH THE WILL OF GOD abideth for ever. LITTLE CHILDREN, IT IS THE LAST TIME: and as ye have heard that antichrist shall come, even now are there many antichrists; WHEREBY WE KNOW THAT IT IS THE LAST TIME"** (1 John 2:15-18). Inasmuch as all these multiplied denominations are opposed to the plain Bible truth of Christ's personal reign on the earth, THEY ARE ANTICHRIST.

John saw **"a sea of glass mingled with fire: and them that had gotten the victory over the beast, and over his image, and over his mark, and over the number of his name, stand on the sea of glass, having the harps of God"** (Revelation 15:2). The Greek word ARITHMOS, here translated "number," is also thus defined, a mob, a worthless multitude, a herd; and some have suggested that these sects make up the number of six hundred threescore and six, which is ascribed to the Antichrist beast; and I confess that the idea of getting the victory over the WORTHLESS MULTITUDE of the beast, looks to me far more consistent, and far more likely to be ascribed by inspiration to the mind that hath wisdom and understanding, than the usual idea of getting the victory over the Hebrew, Greek, Roman letters whose numerical value amounts to 666.

These various Protestant sects have no occasion to take credit to themselves, on account of their professed desires to converting the world to Christ, for the pope is as loud in His professions of this sort as they, and far more consistent and persevering and efficient in his efforts. But altogether Catholics and Protestants are determined on a spiritual reign, and each hopes in their fabled millennium, to be the predominating sect.

If, by the way, either of these sects were to rule the world, it might as well be the Catholics as either, inasmuch as sects have always grown carnal and corrupt, in proportion as their power and influence and wealth have increased; and there is not a sect among them all, but would unquestionably become as corrupt and as cruel and tyrannical as the Catholics ever were, by the time they had gained the same summit of greatness to which the Catholics did once obtain. There is not the sect nor the individual on earth that is worthy of being trusted with irresponsible power.

Many a sect, if told that they would become as wicked as the Catholics ever were, when once they should have the power, would be ready to exclaim with one of old, "**are we dogs that we should do these things?**" (2 Kings 8:13), and yet like him, when once the power should be in their hands, would go straight forward and do them. None is worthy to reign over this world but Christ—none else has a right to reign, and he is coming in the clouds of heaven for that very purpose; while the whole professed Christian world, Catholic and Protestant, are determined that it shall be only a spiritual reign, when each particular sect is hoping to have the ascendancy.

One most unscriptural feature of all their plans is to have the world given to a generation of Christians who have never known anything but peace and safety, while the Bible says if we suffer we shall reign with Him; that we are **"heirs of God, and joint heirs with Christ, if so be that we suffer with Him, that we may be glorified together"** (Romans 8:17); that **"Blessed are they which are persecuted for righteousness' sake: for theirs is the kingdom of heaven"** (Matthew 5:10); that through much tribulation we must enter into the kingdom of God; that those which were beheaded for the witness of Jesus, and the word of Christ, and these John heard singing praise and saying, **"Thou hast made us unto our God kings and priests: and we shall reign on the earth"** (Revelation 5:10).

Notwithstanding all these Scripture declarations respecting those who are to reign with Christ, when the kingdoms of the world are His, and He shall reign forever and ever, it is now claimed that those shall possess the world and reign WITHOUT Christ, who shall be born and live in a time of universal peace, and never have a hair plucked from their heads by way of suffering for Christ's sake. There is no language that can express the immeasurable folly of such pretended Biblical expositions as these. They are immeasurable nonsense. Again, all these pretended Christian sects, are particularly opposed to the idea that Christ is coming SPEEDILY in person, to take the dominion of the world; and ESPECIALLY to the idea that there is Bible evidence for believing that He will come during the present Jewish year. Against this they can find no words to express their indignation.

If it could be deferred a thousand years or so, the idea might be endured. But to think that anybody should believe that Christ is coming the present year to take His seat on David's throne forever, this is intolerable. In these particulars, therefore, the professed Christian world, Catholic and Protestant, are ANTICHRIST. They will not submit to Christ's personal reign in the world. They will not love His appearing, and especially not at present.

Said a professed minister of the gospel, in the state of New Jersey, "If Christ is coming to reign in this world, I'll not stay with Him." Said another minister in the state of Ohio, "God has no right to destroy the world at present. He has no right to make it to be destroyed at such a time." These men were all indulging the very spirit of Antichrist. Thus I have defined what Babylon, or Antichrist, is. It is everything that rises in opposition to the personal reign of Christ on David's throne, and to the revealed time for His appearing, and here we do find the professed Christian world, Catholic and Protestant, on the side of Antichrist. They all say, let US take the kingdom, and let Christ, and the departed saints that have suffered with Him, to whom the kingdom has been promised, remain where they are.

2. What are we to understand by the fall of Babylon?

This is fully expressed in Scriptural language: "**Babylon The Great Is Fallen, Is Fallen, AND IS BECOME THE HABITATION OF DEVILS, AND THE HOLD OF EVERY FOUL SPIRIT, AND A CAGE OF EVERY UNCLEAN AND HATEFUL BIRD**" (Revelation 18:2). Babylon is fallen into this dreadful state. No Protestant sect would think this language too strong to express the true state of things in the Catholic Church at the present time; and the Catholics in their turn would say the same things of Protestants. We need not stop to show how the language applies to Catholicism. The justice of the application is sufficiently obvious.

But how is it with Protestant Christendom? How is she occupied? Is she not engaged, for her own aggrandizement, in every species of merchandise ascribed to Babylon, even to slaves and the souls of men? The spirit of oppression reigns, in greater or less portions of the leading sects unrebuked; and a man may sell or buy his fellow-man, and then sit at the communion table, or even minister at the altar of God, and by the mass of the Protestant Christendom go unreproved. Lust for power is seen among all the sects, and lust for gold is practically regarded by the multitude of Christ's professed disciples as a virtue, and they may resort to any means for acquiring wealth, which does not amount to positive transgression of human law, and yet stand in the church as accredited members. Things in this respect, in the professed church, are entirely the reverse of what they were when as many as were possessors of houses and lands sold them to be distributed for the advancement of the cause of Christ. Sumptuous dwellings and apparel, and equipage, are sought after by professed disciples of the meek and lowly JESUS, as though they were the supreme good; and you will see multitudes of such pretended Christians puffing and strutting about the world in their proud and lofty bearing, and looking down upon the humble followers of the crucified Nazarene, (who dares be singular enough to carry out the principles of the religion of the cross) as though they could find no language sufficient to express their contempt. Speak to them about the coming of Christ to take possession of His throne, and they show themselves sufficiently disgusted to spit in your face.

Ask them to read anything on the subject, and they put on every possible expression of scorn. Even pretended ministers of the gospel, in multitudes, manifested all these feelings in relation to the coming and kingdom of Christ, and do their utmost to perpetuate and increase this state of feeling in their hearers. Mention to them the probability of Christ's coming in His glory during the present Jewish year, to take the throne of the world; and express to them your belief that the Bible fully teaches this, and they feel insulted that you should dare to mention in their presence a thing to them so utterly contemptible. They are ready to hold their breath and thrust you from them as with a pair of tongs.

Ask them if they have ever examined the Bible evidence of the immediate coming of the Lord, and they evidently feel degraded that you should think them capable of turning their thoughts to such a subject. Who are these mighty sons of pride, that God Almighty must not presume to speak to them through His Word? Why they are the professed disciples and ministers of Christ; but in truth and reality Antichrist. They are Babylon in its fallen state; their hearts are the habitation of devils, the hold of every foul spirit, the cage of every unclean and hateful bird. They are in their own estimation of vast consequence, but if they remain what they are a little longer, Jesus will neither be afraid nor ashamed to smite them with the rod of His mouth, and with the breath of His lips to slay them. Many of them may be ready to inquire, **"Lord, Lord, have we not prophesied in thy name? and in thy name have cast out devils? and in thy name done many wonderful works?"** (Matthew 7:22). But Christ will only **"profess unto them, I never knew you: depart from Me, ye that work iniquity"** (Matthew 7:23).

3. What is it for God's people to come out of Babylon?

"Come out of her, my people, that ye be not partakers of her sins, and that ye receive not of her plagues" (Revelation 18:4). To come out of Babylon, is to be converted to the true Scriptural doctrine of the personal coming and kingdom of Christ; to receive the truth on this subject with all readiness of mind, as you find it plainly written out on the pages of the Bible, to love Christ's appearing and rejoice in it, and fully and faithfully to avow to the world your unshrinking belief in God's Word touching this momentous subject, and to do all in your power to open the eyes of others and influence them to a similar course, that they may be ready to meet their Lord. Christ has said, **"Whosoever therefore shall be ashamed of me and of my words in this adulterous and sinful generation; of him also shall the Son of man be ashamed, when he cometh in the glory of his Father with the holy angels"** (Mark 8:38).

Who are you that you should be ashamed of what God has written in His Word respecting the kingdom of Christ, and that you should wish to spiritualize it into some other meaning than God has expressed, for the purpose of making it more popular with those that fear not God? Stand up before the world and dare honestly to avow your belief in what the Almighty God has spoken. Give up "**the lust of the flesh, and the lust of the eye, and the pride of life**" (1 John 2:16); wean yourself from the love of "**this present world**" (Titus 2:12) and be "**looking for that blessed hope, and the glorious appearing of the great God and our Saviour Jesus Christ**" (Titus 2:13). Be just as ready also, to receive and confess all that God has been pleased to reveal, touching the time of the establishment of the kingdom of Christ, as any other part of the subject. Why be ashamed of the time of Christ's coming?

Many are beginning to say, "We are satisfied that the usual notion about a spiritual kingdom of Christ and that the coming of Christ is doubtless near;" but they feel a very great reluctance either to express or to hold any belief respecting the TIME. It is very popular not to know anything about it, and a very convenient way of escaping reproach to be able to say, "We know nothing about it." Thousands are glad that they don't know anything about it, and are very fully determined they will continue to know nothing about it; and some though they profess to have examined the subject, are hindered from the light respecting the time, by the conviction that if they receive the light they must avow it, and this will subject them to reproach. To escape reproach, therefore, they sulk away and hide themselves in darkness. Shame on these miserable sulkers. How will they bear the blazing light of Christ's face at His glorious appearing? They will want rocks and mountains to hide them in that hour. But this time many will begin to say with a sneer of contempt, "You are trying to make it out that none but Millerites can be saved."

Hold one moment, for your soul's sake, and tell if you can, how he can be prepared for the kingdom of Christ, who is opposed to Christ's reigning in person on the throne which God has sworn to give Him, and who is ashamed to believe and avow what God has revealed touching the time of Christ's appearing? If you can see any way into the kingdom of God for such a soul as that, I frankly confess you can see what I cannot. Do you still complain that I should try to make it appear that you are not a Christian? I have no such desire. I pray God that you may make it appear that you are a Christian. But I do say, if you are a Christian, COME OUT OF BABYLON. If you intend to be found a Christian when Christ appears, COME OUT OF BABYLON, and come out NOW.

Throw away that miserable medley of ridiculous spiritualizing nonsense, with which multitudes have so long been making the Word of God of none effect, and dare to believe the Bible. It contains the wisdom of the infinite God as it is, and needs no alterations and emendation from men, as though they could tell what God means better than He has been able to express it in His own language. "**He has sworn with an oath that he would raise up the seed of David to sit on David's throne**" (Acts 2:30) and "**THE KINGDOMS OF THIS WORLD shall become the kingdoms of our Lord and of His Christ, and He shall reign FOREVER AND EVER**" (Revelation 11:15).

And now away forever with your miserable transcendental philosophy, that would make the throne of David a spiritual throne, and the coming of Christ to sit upon it a spiritual coming, and His reign a spiritual reign. Thanks be to God, His kingdom cannot be blown up into such spiritual bubbles as these, for a thousand, or even 365 thousand years, and then blown forever away into some etherial something, which some sneering infidel has defined, to be sitting on a cloud and singing Psalms to all eternity. No, no. Jesus Christ has been raised up in David's flesh immortalized, and He shall come in that flesh glorified, "**and there shall be given unto Him dominion, and glory, and a kingdom, that all people, nations, and languages, should serve Him: His dominion is an everlasting dominion, which shall not**

pass away, and His kingdom that which shall not be destroyed" (Daniel 7:14). "**And the kingdom and dominion, and the greatness of the kingdom under the whole heaven, shall be given to the people of the saints of the most High:**" "**and the saints of the most High shall take the kingdom, and possess the kingdom forever, even forever and ever**" (Daniel 7:27, 18).

This is God's Word, and all the spiritualizers on the footstool cannot alter it. They may undertake to tell what God means by it, but God has given His own meaning in His own language, and He will make it good by fulfilling it as He has caused it to be written. If God had meant something else and not this, He would have told us what He did mean. Just as though when God had given us truth in symbolic language, and then interpreted it, that it might be fully understood, He had after all left it for men, in the upstart folly, to improve His own revelation.

My soul is pained when I reflect how the Word of God has been rendered powerless upon the consciences and heart of men by the attempts which have been made to alter it into something else. And now a multitude of ministers of all the multiplied sects of Antichrist will begin to say, "Thus saying, Thou reproachest us also," and will perhaps accuse me of dealing in wholesale denunciation, when I refuse to acknowledge them to be the true ministers of Christ. All I have to say is, if you are the true ministers of Christ, COME OUT OF BABYLON, and no longer be opposed to the coming of Christ, as the Bible declares He will come, to take His seat forever on the throne which God has sworn to Give Him. I do not say that you and your hearers may not have been converted to Christ; but I do say, if you have, it remains for you to show it by coming out of Babylon and by standing no longer opposed to the reign of Jesus. God never will alter His Word to suit your carnal desires. He has written it, and as He has written He will fulfill it, and if you are ashamed of it, He will be ashamed of you. Dare you believe the Bible? Dare you preach it? Dare you bring out its plain testimony respecting the manner, the objects, and the time of Christ's coming, and tell the world that it is truth, and meet the consequences? Or will you turn away with a sneer and call it Millerism; and go on prating about a spiritual reign of Christ? I tell you, if you continue in that course you will be reckoned with Antichrist, when the glorious Son of David comes to take His throne. "**Come out of her, My people, that ye be not partakers of her sins, and that ye receive not of her plagues**" (Revelation 18:4).

4. It remains that I speak of the consequences of refusing to come out of Babylon.

God declares her downfall, and foretells her destruction in time to give all His people who may be in her, an opportunity to come out and escape; and then, as a mighty angel would cast a millstone into the sea, God will cast down Babylon, and she shall be found no more at all. And now many will begin to say, "If I confess my belief in the personal reign of Christ, and that the reign is immediately to commence, I shall lose my reputation, my influence, my friends, my all that I value on earth." And has not Christ said that you must do this? Has He not positively declared, "**Whosoever he be of you that forsaketh not all that he hath, he cannot be my disciple**" (Luke 14:33).

Do you say, "I did that years ago, and have been acquiring friends and reputation since, and did not expect to be called upon to lay these down"? And because you have taken up the cross once, do you claim that that ought to be sufficient, and that it is too hard to do it for Christ a second time? Has not Christ said, in Luke 9:23, "**If any man will come after Me, let him deny himself, and take up his cross DAILY, and follow Me**"?

Having once sacrificed all for Christ, have you now acquired something which is too dear to be given up for Him? Is it not he that

ENDURETH the cross, to the end, and that denies himself daily, that shall be saved? So you begin to say, "I acquired this reputation for Christ, and hoped to use it for Him, and that it is now hard to part with it?" Very well, then show your sincerity by being willing to sacrifice it for Christ when He calls. If you sought the birth of Isaac that God might be glorified in him, then be willing to offer Isaac on God's altar, that God may be glorified the more. Remember, you can never glorify God in the use of that which you are unwilling God should take away. You will never use anything for God's glory which you do not hold perfectly and continually at God's disposal.

It is not for you and me to say whether we will have reputation or not; but it is for us to say whether we will please God or not; and having done this, let the Lord decide what our reputation shall be. This He has decided already, that we shall have our names cast out as evil for His sake, and in this we ought ever to rejoice. Will you then, professed disciples of Jesus Christ, find the truth respecting the coming of the Lord, and hold it up, and leave the results with God?

Friends will be tried and mortified, and feel themselves disgraced by you; your church will call you fanatical and foolish, thus to throw away your influence and curtail your usefulness; Satan will beset you with all manner of temptation and a wicked world will laugh you to scorn; but can you not endure as much as this for Him who has endured ten thousand times more for you? Just remember then what must be the consequences of refusing to receive the truth and to abide by it. Babylon must be destroyed, and you with it. But, say a multitude of professed ministers and Christians, "I don't expect to be damned just because I don't believe in Millerism." Now don't let the devil cheat you out of heaven through your fears of bearing a single epithet of reproach. Does the Bible teach the personal coming of Christ to sit on David's throne? Has the Spirit of Christ, which was in the prophets,

SIGNIFIED A TIME, when it spake before of the sufferings of Christ and OF THE GLORY THAT SHOULD FOLLOW? So Peter has taught.

If you dare believe God, find out His truth on this subject, and hold it up to the world. If you hate the appearing of Christ, if you are opposed to His reigning personally over the earth after God has sworn that He shall, if you are afraid or ashamed to receive and avow the truth on these momentous subjects, then blame not me for saying you are Antichrist. I do not say how many Christians, or how few there are in professed Christendom, but I do say, that in their present attitude or opposition to the personal reign of Christ, they are Antichrist, and that they must abandoned their present position and embrace and defend the truth or go down with Babylon into the bottom of the sea, and rise no more at all to life. They can have no resurrection at all, but to damnation.

To be found at Christ's appearing, as the numerous sects now are, in an attitude of hostility to His personal reign, ashamed to believe and confess what God has revealed as to the manner and time of His coming, must be their ruin. Say not in your heart, I have long been a servant of Christ, and therefore must be safe. He cannot be a faithful servant who, for any reason, hates His Lord's return and wishes it deferred. Nor can you see His face in peace, while fear, or shame, or love of reputation, or anything else, leads you to indulge in any opposition of heart to His immediate appearing.

Come out of Babylon or perish. If you are a Christian stand for Christ, and hold out unto the end. I do not undertake to say how many in these professed Christian sects will be saved or lost, but I hesitate not to say that every individual among them, who is found a true child of God in the end, will cease his opposition to Christ's personal reign, and be found at last faithfully defending the truth. Not one that is ever saved can remain in Babylon.

Do not accuse me of a desire to cut you off from salvation. My only desire is to show you your danger, that I may induce you to hasten your escape; but take care I beseech you, that you do not cut yourself off by remaining in Babylon.

Do you say, "I am willing that Christ should reign as He pleases?" Are you willing so to embrace Christ and His truth, and so to let your light shine as to meet and unshrinkingly bear the cross? The offense of the cross has not ceased in the case of those who will avow and defend God's truth; though it must be confessed that in the popular religion of the day, there is no such thing as self-denial; and this fact of itself proves that it is not the religion of Jesus. But cast off this ungodly world, carry out the religion of Jesus in all its principles, and from the Bible defend His personal coming in manner and time, His personal and eternal reign, and do your duty in seeking to induce others to prepare for it, and you will not be long in finding the cross. Thus may the Lord help you, reader, "**to come out of Babylon and be no more a partaker of her sins, that you receive not of her plagues**" (Revelation 18:4). *AMEN*.

NOTE: The growing conviction of various Second Advent preachers and laymen that they should no longer stay in their respective churches, now was reinforced in 1843 by a solemn Scriptural command: "Come out of her, My people." Fitch's views quickly took hold of many minds. His sermon was published first in the *Second Advent* paper in Cleveland, Ohio, of which he was the editor. IT WAS SOON REPUBLISHED AS A PAMPHLET. A little later the prominent S*econd Advent* publication in New York printed the sermon in full, explaining that the "call for it has been so great that we have inserted it in *The Midnight Cry*."

The great principles of the Bible never change.

Letters

by Charles Fitch
From *The Midnight Cry*, March 14,1844

LETTER ONE

Cleveland,Ohio
February 24, 1844.

Dear Brethren of The Midnight Cry,

Our dear Brother Storrs says that **the Great Head of the Church designed that we should come out of Babylon, and not wait for Babylon to thrust us out**. I believe he is right, and I am therefore determined to come out.

Subsequently to my being separated from the Newark Presbytery, I was induced, at the solicitation of several clergymen, to unite with the New York Congregational Association, and was received by that body, and became a subscriber to its creed: having also been received by the General Association of the Western Reserve.

This is now nearly three years since. I have never met with them since that time, and do not know whether they retain my name among their list of members or not. But I now wish to say through your paper to the world, **that I do from this time regard myself, and hereby proclaim myself to all men, as free and independent of all ecclesiastical domination, as a member of no sect, and a subscriber to no creed.** At the same time, I received the Bible as the Word of the Living God, and am looking for the immediate coming of the Lord Jesus Christ, to whom I must give account.

"**Grace, mercy, and peace, from God our Father and Jesus Christ our Lord**" (1 Timothy 1:2) to all who love Him in sincerity; and love to all who love His appearing.

Yours in the blessed hope,
CHARLES FITCH

LETTER TWO

Cleveland, Ohio
February 24, 1844

Dear Brother,

With regard to the cause of truth in this region, it is progressing against great opposition. I have just returned from Painsville, where I have had a delightful season. Congregations large and attentive.

I was cheered by being taken by the hand, time after time, and told, "You were the means of leading me to Christ when you were here a year ago." The Lord be praised.

On the last evening I was with them, we celebrated the Lord's Supper. A large number, Congregational, Presbyterian, Methodist, and Disciples, together, remembered the Lord in that blessed ordinance, in obedience to His command. My wife and myself have recently been "buried with Christ by baptism;" having received that precious ordinance at the hands of Brother Cook. I have since baptized about thirty in Cleveland, and eight at Painsville. The most of them have been members of Churches. Brother Pickands and wife, and a large number of his church, have also been baptized. The state of things among his people is truly delightful. They are a happy band, looking without wavering for the coming of the Lord. We have much more opposition to contend with than we had a year ago, but we do not forget that he which endureth unto the end shall be saved, and that opposition is the very thing which we are called upon to endure.

Brother Himes wrote me, some time since, to spend a week at Buffalo, and the brethren at Rochester wish me to attend a conference with them. I intend to do so, as soon as navigation opens on the lake. Till then, the great necessity of making constant efforts here, the urgent calls for labor in the region, and the great difficulty of making a journey of two hundred miles by land just at the breaking up of the roads, will confine me to this state.

In this place I have found the same necessity for constant effort that our brethren have found in the eastern cities. Multitudes stand ready to devour, and wait, eager to find some pretext for saying that the lovers of the Lord's appearing are giving up their faith, and that the cause of the Adventist is going down.

It has, therefore, been necessary that I labor statedly at Cleveland, and go abroad when practicable. This I have been endeavoring to do in the midst of sickness and death in my family, and other afflictions, and the determined opposition, contempt, and scorn of those who hate the truth of the Lord's immediate appearing.

My whole being cries out, "**Come, Lord Jesus**" (Revelation 22:20). Take Thy great power and reign. I tremble in myself, when I think of meeting Him that trieth the reins of the heart. Still I know that I love His appearing, and feel a confidence in His mercy, that He will not cast me out.

Yours in the blessed and glorious hope,
CHARLES FITCH

LETTER THREE

From *The Midnight Cry,*
Dec. 21, 1843

Dear Brother Himes:

This day I have laid in the grave my dear Willie, a little boy that would have been seven years of age the 15th of the present month. I need not tell you that my heart aches, and I cannot tell you how much. Some ten months ago, he took an inflammatory rheumatism, which left him with an organic disease of the heart. He was comfortable through the summer, and went east with us. He kept about until the last of October. While I was absent at that time, he was prostrated. On my return the physicians said there was no hope of his recovery. Oh, how my heart was pained at the prospects of seeing his life wrung out of him with anguish, of then following him away to the cold grave.

I stood and watched by his side three weeks, held him in my arms to relieve his distress, and sung to him at his oft repeated request the second advent hymns to beguile his tedious hours. "Sing to me, Pa," was his repeated request every hour. "What shall I sing, my dear?" "Sing, *How Long O Lord Our Saviour,*" and again, "sing, *Lo, What a Glorious Sight Appears,* sing, *My Faith Looks Up to Thee.*" After three weeks, I thought he might live for weeks to come, and feeling it to be duty, I tore myself away from his side with an aching heart, and I went last Monday week to Huron county to preach the kingdom of the Lord. On Sabbath morning last, being in Fairfield, more than 60 miles from home, I was awakened from my pillow by a messenger who said, "Your child is dead." I hastened home, and we have just laid him in his lowly bed. It has been painful, painful; but the Lord sustains us. But we have hope in his death.

When he was three years of age, I was accustomed to relate to him in language suited to his capacity, the interesting incidents in the life of our Saviour, for the purpose of teaching him to know and love the character of Christ. He became exceedingly interested, and would often climb my knee and say, "Now, Pa, tell me something about the blessed Saviour." At length he arose from his bed one morning very early, and came to me, calling my name repeatedly to get my attention as I was conversing. He said, "The blessed Saviour is my Saviour." This was said by him, when there had been nothing at that time to turn his attention to the subject. Sweeter accents than those never fell upon my ear. Never from that moment did his faith in Jesus waiver. When told by a sister some years older than himself, "You will never live to be a man. The Saviour is coming soon, and the world will be burned," he replied, "I don't care, the Saviour will take care of me."

Once when he saw me greatly disquieted at some perplexing circumstances which came suddenly upon me, and at which I ought not to have been moved, he said, in his usual calm and deliberate manner, "The Saviour will come pretty soon, and then we shan't have any more trouble."

In his sickness, he manifested the most perfect resignation. During all the time I was with him, he never expressed a desire to get well, or to be relieved from suffering. At one time when I had expressed such a desire, he replied, "The Saviour can make me well if He wants me well." He had his senses till the last, knew perfectly well he was dying, composed himself, closed his own eyes, and died with as much calmness, as he would have gone in health to his pillow for a night's repose.

He was not without the follies and faults of childhood, but we do believe he lived and died with confidence in Christ, and we cannot doubt that the blessed Saviour is indeed Willie's Saviour.

Perhaps I should apologize for occupying you with so much that has no particular interest for any but ourselves, but when our bosoms are heaving with sighs we cannot suppress, and our eyes are gushing with tears which will flow, we love to lay open our whole hearts to those we know have hearts to feel. I must not neglect to say, that we have had friends through all our affliction, that have been friends indeed.

CHARLES FITCH

Appendix

The Power of the Gospel.

A

DISCOURSE,

PREACHED JUNE 20th, 1841,

BY CHARLES FITCH,

IN REVIEW OF A SERMON BY

REV. OTIS A. SKINNER,

AT THE INSTALLATION OF

REV. T. P. ABELL,

OVER THE

UNIVERSALIST SOCIETY,

HAVERHILL, MASS.

HAVERHILL:
FROM THE ESSEX BANNER PRESS.
1841.

The Power of the Gospel

Romans 1:16

For I am not ashamed of the gospel of Christ;
for it is the power of God unto salvation to every one that believeth;
to the Jew first, and also to the Greek.

The object of this discourse is, to discharge a solemn duty, both to God and men - to God, that His name may be glorified, and to men, that their souls may be saved. In relation to my fellow men, I can truly say, that "I seek not mine own profit, but the profit of many that they may be saved." And also, that "my hearts desire and prayer to God" for every man "is that he may be saved."

I was passing the Universalist Church, in this village, the other day, at a time when an installation service was in progress, and after revolving in my own mind the question, whether I would be likely to get good, or to do good by attending such a service, I was led, as I trust, by the Spirit of God to enter.

After listening to the discourse which was preached on the occasion, and to the other services, I remembered the words of God to the prophet Ezekiel, contained in the third chapter of the writings of that prophet. "Son of man, I have made thee a watchman to the house of Israel; therefore hear the word at my mouth, and give them warning from me. When I say unto the wicked, thou shalt surely die; and thou givest him not warning, nor speakest to warn the wicked from his wicked way to save his life, the same wicked man shall die in his iniquity: but his blood will I require at thine hand. Yet if thou warn the wicked, and he turn not from his wickedness, nor from his wicked way; he shall die in his iniquity, but thou hast delivered thy soul."

Again, "when a righteous man doth turn from his righteousness and commit iniquity, and I lay a stumbling block before him, he shall die because thou hast not given him warning, he shall die in his sin, and his righteousness which he hath done shall not be remembered; but his blood will I require at thine hand. Nevertheless if thou warn the righteous man, that the righteous sin not, and he doth not sin, he shall surely live, because he is warned: Also thou hast delivered thy soul." In the thirty-third chapter of the same prophet, we read as follows: "Again the word of the Lord came unto me, saying, Son of man, speak to the children of my people, and say unto them, When I bring the sword upon a land, if the people of the land take a man of their coasts and set him for a watchman; If when he see the sword come upon the land, he blow the trumpet and warn the people, then whosoever heareth the sound of the trumpet, and taketh not warning, if the sword come and take him away, his blood shall be upon his own head. He heard the sound of the trumpet and took not warning, his blood shall be upon him; but he that taketh warning shall deliver his soul. But if the watchman see the sword come, and blow not the trumpet, and the people be not warned; if the sword come and take any person from among them, he is taken away in his iniquity; but his blood will I require at the watchman's hand. So thou, O son of man, I have set thee a watchman unto the House of Israel; therefore thou shalt hear the word at my mouth and warn them from me. When I say unto the wicked, 0 wicked man thou shalt surely die; if thou dost not speak to warn the wicked from his way, that wicked man shall die in his iniquity but his blood will I require at thine hand. Nevertheless if thou warn the wicked of his way to turn from it, if he does not turn from his way, he shall die in his iniquity, but thou hast delivered thy soul." Now God has made me a watchman for the welfare of souls. To Him I stand accountable. No man can deliver me from responsibility in relation to his soul. If I see danger, and can make my voice beard, and warn him not, God has said, "his blood will I require at thine hand." Now I see danger to immortal souls in this community, by the efforts which are made to persuade men to the belief of the doctrine of Universal Salvation; and it is the voice of God that calls me, and the authority of God that commands me to lift the note of warning. Many may refuse to hear, but I must obey God and deliver my own soul, by endeavoring faithfully and plainly, yet affectionately, to lift the note of warning.

The discourse to which I allude was preached from the words which I have placed at the head of this. "For I am not ashamed of the gospel of Christ; for it is the power of God unto salvation, to every one that believeth." The object of the preacher was, to show in what the power of the Gospel consisted.

From the commencement, he assumed it as the design of the gospel, to save men from sin, and thereby prepare them for heaven; and it was therefore his object to show in what the power of the gospel to save men consisted.

Now, that the preacher was right in his assumption, that it is the design of the gospel to save men from sin, I am fully prepared to admit. I believe it may have been true, in some cases, at least, that this grand truth has been kept out of sight; while the gospel has been held forth as rather a way of salvation from hell, than from sin. Now he who is saved from sin and preserved blameless, will unquestionably find an immortality of bliss, for our Lord Jesus Christ has said, "Blessed are the pure in heart, for they shall see God." We also find the following in the book of Psalms: "Who shall ascend into the hill of the Lord? and who shall stand in His holy place? He that hath clean hands and

a pure heart," Let a man therefore be saved from sin, and the blessedness of his soul is sure; and equally true is it, that he who is not saved
from sin, can never inherit the kingdom of God, "for there shall in no
wise enter therein anything that defileth, neither whatsoever worketh
abomination or maketh a lie." We also learn that the design of the gospel is to save men from their sin, by the words of God to his ancient
people Israel, respecting the object of that ceremonial worship, which
was designed to point out Christ, and the end of his coming into the
world. Lev. l6: 30. "For on that day shall the priest make atonement for
you to cleanse you, that ye may be clean from all your sins before the
Lord." This idea of cleansing was ever kept in view in all that system of
ceremonial worship—while the grand design of that system was to set
forth Christ and the object of his coming into the world. Accordingly
we are told by Paul, in his Epistle to the Hebrews, that these rites and
ceremonies "were a figure for the time then present, in which were
offered both gifts and sacrifices which could not make him that did
the service, nor the comers thereunto perfect, as pertaining to the con-
science, which stood only in meats and drinks and divers washings
and carnal ordinances imposed on them until the time of reformation.
But Christ being come a high priest of good things to come, by a greater and more perfect tabernacle, not made with hands, that is to say,
not of this building; neither by the blood of goats and calves, but by
His own blood; he entered in once into the holy place, having obtained
eternal redemption for us. For if the blood of bulls and of goats and the
ashes of an heifer sprinkling the unclean sanctifieth to the purifying of
the flesh; how much more shall the blood of Christ, who through the
Eternal Spirit offered himself without spot to God, purge your con-
science from dead works to serve the living God. And for this cause,"
i.e. for the purpose of purging us from dead works to serve the living
God, "he is the Mediator of the New Testament." And we are told in the

same epistle, what that New Testament is. "I will put my laws in their minds and write them in their hearts." As if to say, ye shall not be as were the Jews in the time of Christ, like whited sepulchres, beautiful indeed without, but full of all uncleanness within. "The Lord thy God will circumcise thy heart, to love the Lord thy God with all thy heart, and with all thy soul, that thou mayest live." It is therefore held forth in every part of the bible as the design of the salvation of the Gospel, to set men free from sin, and when they are thus effectually saved, there cannot be a doubt that they will find their blessedness here and hereafter in communion with God, as surely as he is a God of purity and love. Accordingly the angel that foretold the birth of our Saviour said, "Thou shall call his name Jesus," i.e. a Saviour, "for he shall save his people from their sins." Hence, also, we hear God saying, "Behold I will bring forth out of Zion the Deliverer, and he shall turn away ungodliness from Jacob. For this is my covenant with them when I shall take away their sins." I greatly rejoice, that it is beginning to be recognized more and more, as the great design of the gospel to make men pure and holy, and thereby "meet to be partakers of the inheritance of the saints in light." The danger on this point is, that men shall think themselves cleansed by the gospel, while in the sight of God they are still altogether unclean; or shall regard themselves as so sure of being cleansed at last, that they shall pass on uncleansed, until they die in their iniquities, and consequently find, that "where Christ has gone they never can come."

I know it has sometimes been said of Universalists, that they maintain that men of all characters will be taken to Heaven. This charge is manifestly false. They believe that all men will become holy, and then be received to heaven; and I rejoice to admit, that in assuming it as the grand and glorious design of the gospel, to save men from sin, they hold forth a sentiment which harmonizes with the whole tenor of sacred scripture. The fatal mistake which they embrace, is on another point, as I expect hereafter to show. The Preacher of the sermon in question, in proceeding to show in what consisted the power of the gospel' to save men from sin, remarked,

I. Negatively; that it did not consist, 1. In propitiatory worship. This he stated was t,he design of all heathen worship, and conveyed, as I understood him, the idea, that such worship was no ,better than heathenism. Now that men need a propitiatory sacrifice, in coming to God with acceptance, is very evident from the fact, that the bible teaches us, that Christ is the propitiation for our sins, and not for ours only but also for the sins of the whole world. If therefore no propitiation had been necessary, God, certainly would never have provided one. But Christ, is ever to be regarded as an all sufficient propitiation: and I am fully prepared to admit, that if we bring before God any works or offerings of our own, as a propitiation, our worship must be no better in his sight than the worship of Pagans. For God has provided a propitiation that is all sufficient, and if I attempt to bring another, I treat that which God has offered as of no value, and set up some works or sacrifices of my own, as more meritorious than those of Christ in my behalf, which is unquestionably mocking God, and treating with the greatest possible indignity the Saviour whom he has sent into the world. I am to cast away all dependence on myself, and make the propitiation of Christ all my hope, and come with an unwavering faith therein, and then I honor the Saviour whom God has provided. But whether I bring a propitiation of my own, or say that no propitiation is needed, or place no confidence in that which God has provided, I do equally set at nought the propitiation of Christ.

The preacher remarked 2. That the power of the Gospel did not consist in mysteries. On this point I have only to remark, that the bible declares "great is the mystery of Godliness," and also speaks of "the riches of the glory of this mystery, which is Christ in us the hope of glory."

He also said 3. That the power of the gospel did not consist in human learning. On this point I have nothing to say but to assent.

He remarked 4th. That the power of the gospel did not consist in the doctrine of endless punishment. On this point I readily admit, that a mere belief in the doctrine of endless punishment, never did, never will save a man from sin. I have no doubt that many a sinner has lived and died in the belief of that doctrine, and been lost forever, and that many others will follow in the same course, loving their sins too well to renounce them, though fully aware that the end of the wicked must be "everlasting destruction from the presence of the Lord and from the glory of his power." At the same time I know it to be a fact, that the doctrine of endless punishment has often been used by the Holy Spirit to arrest the sinner in his course of iniquity, and to lead him to seek a way of salvation from sin, though a mere belief in that doctrine has never saved any man, and never will. I think no candid mind will deny that to set clearly before a transgressor the certain consequences of his evil courses, has some tendency to restrain him, and to influence him to look after a way of safety. But it is admitted freely, that the *power* of the gospel to save men from sin does not consist in the doctrine of endless punishment.

The Preacher then proceeded to show

II. In what the power of the gospel to save from sin, did consist; and stated that it consisted, 1st. In the love of God. 2d. In the doctrine of a common brotherhood. 3d. In the nature of its punishment. 4th. In the doctrine or hope of life and immortality.

Now the fundamental and fatal mistake of the preacher consisted, as I expect to show, from the bible, not so much in what he did say, as in what he did not say. I freely admit the influence of the love of God in saving men from sin; and that if ever saved from sin, it will be in loving God because He first loved us. I admit the influence of that new command of Christ, which requires all men to love one another as He has loved them. I admit that the punishment of the *Gospel* is disciplinary, yielding the peaceable fruits of righteousness to them which are exercised thereby and consequently reformatory, and inflicted only in the present life; while the punishment of the future life which the bible calls the second death, is retributive, i.e. meted out to all that cannot be reclaimed by the love of God, according to their works.

But that there will be those who will never be reclaimed from sin by the love of God, we learn from the bible when it speaks as in the second chap. of the 2d Epist. to the Thess. of "them that perish, because they receive not the love of the truth that they might be saved. And that for this cause God shall send them strong delusion to believe a lie that they all might be damned who believed not the truth but bad pleasure in unrighteousness." The bible also speaks of those who know not "that the goodness of God leadeth them to repentance; but after their hardness and impenitent heart, treasure up unto themselves wrath, against the day of wrath, and revelation of the righteous judgment of God."

I come now to the main design of this discourse, which is to show that the Preacher to whom I allude, has entirely failed to show in what the power of the gospel to save men from sin does consist. He has not even alluded in all the points which he has named, to that, without which, the gospel ever has been and ever will be, of none effect.

The apostle Paul tells us in what the power of the gospel consists, when he says as in the first chapter of his 1st Epistle to the Thessalonians, "For our gospel came not unto you in word only, but in *power and in the Holy Ghost.*" Peter in the first chapter of his 1st Epistle, speaks of "the things which were reported by them that have preached the gospel, *with the Holy Ghost sent down from Heaven.*"

Paul also says to Titus. "Not by works of righteousness which we have done, but according to His mercy He saved us, i.e. from sin, *"by the washing of regeneration and renewing of the Holy Ghost* which He shed on us abundantly through Jesus Christ our Savior." The power of the gospel then to save from sin, consists in the re generating, renewing, and sanctifying influences of the Spirit of God, shell forth to attend the gospel through Jesus Christ our Savior, and without these influences, the Gospel with all the love which it reveals, is utterly powerless, in working in the hearts of men, that "holiness, without which no man shall see the Lord."

Accordingly our Lord Jesus Christ at his ascension, after having commissioned his disciples to go into all the world and preach the gospel to every creature, commanded them not to depart from Jerusalem, but to wait for the promise of the Father. "Ye shall receive power," said He, "After that the Holy Ghost is come upon you, and ye shall be witnesses unto me both in Jerusalem and in all Judea and in Samaria and unto the uttermost parts of the earth."

Having therefore received from Christ the direction, "tarry ye in the city of Jerusalem, *until ye be endued with power from on high*, and the assurance behold I send the promise of my Father upon you; and ye shall receive power, after that the Holy Ghost is come upon you, the disciples returned unto Jerusalem from the Mount called Olivet, which is from Jerusalem a Sabbath day's journey, and went into an upper chamber, and there continued with one accord in prayer and supplication, both men and women, until they were, on the day of Pentecost, all filled with the Holy Ghost. Then they preached the gospel with the Holy Ghost sent down from heaven, and multitudes were pricked in their hearts and inquired what shall we do? And when others mocking said these men are full of new wine"-they replied, "this Jesus whom ye crucified hath God raised up whereof we all are witnesses. Therefore being by the right hand of God exalted, and having received of the Father the promise of the Holy Ghost, he hath shed forth this which ye now see and hear. Yea and all the prophets from Samuel and those that follow after have likewise foretold these days. Unto you first, God having raised up his Son Jesus Christ, sent him to bless you, in turning away every one of you from his iniquities." Here then we behold the power of the gospel to save men from sin: It is in being attended by the Holy Ghost sent down from Heaven. I freely admit that it is the setting forth of the love of God which saves men from sin, but in order that the love of God may have its cleansing efficacy—it must be as Paul says to the Romans, "the love of God shed abroad in our hearts by the Holy Ghost which is given unto us." Accordingly we find, that the success of the Apostles in saving men from sin by the preaching of the gospel, is uniformly ascribed to the Holy Ghost. Barnabas was a man full of the Holy Ghost and faith, and much people were added to the Lord. Peter preached at the house of Cornelius, and the Holy Ghost fell on all which heard the word. "Then remembered I," said he, "the word of the Lord, how that he said, John indeed baptised with water, but ye shall be baptised with the Holy Ghost."

The whole current of the New Testament shows that the work which should follow the coming of Christ, should be the dispensation of the Holy Ghost. Peter in the first chapter of his 1st Epistle tells us, that the prophets searched and inquired diligently respecting the time of this salvation, which the Spirit of Christ which was in them signified, when it testified beforehand of the sufferings of Christ and the *glory* that should follow. This glory was to be the outpouring of the Spirit as predicted by Joel; and which Ezekiel also had in view, when God is heard saying by the mouth of that prophet, "then will I sprinkle clean water upon you and ye shall be clean, from all your filthiness and from all your idols will I cleanse you. And I will save you from all your uncleannesses." Here also is brought to view by the prophets that baptism of the Holy Ghost which was to be the establishment of the kingdom of Heaven upon earth—which kingdom we are told is "*righteousness, peace,* and joy in the Holy Ghost."

John the Baptist was sent to prepare the way of the Lord for the establishment of this kingdom. This work of preparation was performed by him, as he preached saying, "Repent ye, for the kingdom of Heaven is at hand, the kingdom of "righteousness, peace, and joy in the Holy Ghost." "I indeed baptise you with water unto repentance, but there cometh one after me, mightier than I, the latchet of whose shoes I am not worthy to unloose, He shall baptise you with the Holy Ghost and with fire. Whose fan is in his hand, and he will thoroughly purge his floor, and gather his wheat into the garner, but be will burn up the chaff with unquenchable fire."

The same great truths Christ himself had in view, when he said to Nicodemus, "Verily verily, I say unto thee, except a man be born of water and of the Spirit-he cannot enter into the kingdom of God." What is the kingdom of God? "Righteousness, peace, and joy in the Holy Ghost., What is it to be born of water? It is to receive John's baptism unto repentance. That is, truly to repent and bring forth fruits meet for repentance. This prepares the way of the kingdom of heaven in us. What is it to be born of the Spirit? It is to receive the baptism of Christ with the Holy Ghost, or to have Christ "sprinkle clean water upon us, and make us clean; and cleanse us from all our filthiness, and from all our idols." Then when this baptism of Christ is received, when this work of purification is wrought by being baptised with the Holy Ghost, we enter that "'kingdom of God" which "is righteousness, peace, and joy in the Holy Ghost." And we have the positive asservation of the Son of God, "Verily, verily, I say unto you except a man be born of water" i.e. led to the exercise of true repentance, "and of the Spirit" i.e. sprinkled with clean water, or baptised with the Holy Ghost, and cleansed from all his filthiness and from all his idols—he cannot enter into the "kingdom of God," which "is righteousness, and peace, and joy in the Holy Ghost."

Here then we clearly see, my hearers, what it is which makes the gospel of Christ the power of God unto salvation from sin. It is Our Lord Jesus Christ, baptising with the Holy Ghost, and thus cleansing men from all their filthiness and from all their idols; thus bringing them into God's kingdom of righteousness, and establishing that kingdom in their hearts—filling them with righteousness, as Christ says those shall be, who hunger and thirst after it; and giving them peace and joy in the Holy Ghost—making their peace as a river and their righteousness as the waves of the sea. This gospel is indeed the power of God unto salvation to every one that believeth. It is the dispensation of God's Almighty Spirit, "Burying us with Jesus Christ, by baptism of the Holy Ghost into death" i.e. making us dead to sin—"that like as Christ was raised up from the dead by the glory of the Father, so we also should walk in newness of life." It is enabling us to "put off the old man which is corrupt according to the deceitful lusts, and to put on the new man, which after God" (i.e. after the likeness of God) "is created in righteousness and true holiness."

REMARKS

1. We may see that while the advocates of Universal Salvation take correct ground, in assuming it as the design of the gospel to save men from sin, they fail entirely of gaining that salvation, by leaving out of the account the work of the Holy Ghost in renewing and cleansing the heart. "Create in me" said the Psalmist "a clean heart, and renew a right spirit within me. Purge me with hyssop and I shall be clean, wash me and I shall be whiter than snow."

Here it is recognized as the work of God to save from sin, to cleanse the heart, while the Universalist expects to cleanse his own heart, by his contemplations of the universal love of God. I know it is by the revelation of the love of God that the heart must be cleansed—but this love as I have already said, great as it is, is powerless on the hearts of men, until "shed abroad in their hearts by the Holy Ghost given unto them." Paul speaks of "the gift of the grace of God given unto him by the effectual working of God's power." It is in this way that every gift of God's grace is communicated: only by the effectual working of God's power. The bible represents unholy men as dead in trespasses and sins, and as having no spiritual life but in Christ. When our first parents ate the forbidden fruit they died a spiritual death, and all their posterity are under the power of that death, and will remain under it forever, unless raised by the power of God. Hence we hear Christ say "I am the resurrection and the life; he that believeth in me though he were dead yet shall he live, and he that liveth and believeth in me shall never die. I am the way and the truth and the life. Except ye eat the flesh of the Son of man and drink his blood, ye have no life in you." He therefore who would have spiritual life is to look to Christ for it. He is to seek, through faith in Christ, that baptism of the Holy Ghost which will cleanse him from sin; or in other words, raise him up from his spiritual death, and make him alive to the love and enjoyment of God. That same God who first breathed into man the breath of spiritual life, so that he became a living soul—must again by the power of that same Spirit breathe spiritual life anew, or the sinner will remain dead in sin forever. All his contemplations of the love of God, without this Baptism of the Holy Ghost, this resurrection from spiritual death by the power of Christ, will avail nothing. Men will by such contemplations, become no better than whited sepulchres. If the outside is beautiful, the uncleanness will all remain within. "If ye believe not that I am he," said Christ "ye shall *die in your sins.*" "And whither I go ye cannot come." If ye believe not that I am who? Why the Savior whom God promised to send into the world; and whose "name was called Jesus, because he should save his people from their sins."

The question then, for you to settle, my hearers, is this. Have you been baptised by the Holy Ghost? Have you been raised up by the power of Christ's spiritual resurrection from the death of sin and made alive unto God, and had that kingdom of God established within you which "is righteousness, peace, and joy in the Holy Ghost." If not you are dead in sin, and your expectation of going where Christ is, in your present state, will avail you nothing. To the Jews, Christ said, ye will not come unto me that ye may have life. Coming to the doctrine of Universal Salvation then, will not cleanse men from sin, and give them spiritual life. They must come to Christ for it by faith, and receive it by the power of the Holy Ghost, for "the kingdom of God is not in word but in power." I beseech you therefore my hearers to abandon all hope of salvation from sin from the doctrine of Universal Salvation. "Why seek ye the living among the dead." " Christ is not there, he is risen."

There is no spiritual life in that system. No baptism of the Holy Ghost. They know not what it means. Christ has never been revealed in them, "the hope of glory." They know nothing about "the riches of the glory of that mystery." They are only expecting to be saved from sin, because all will be; and are not looking to Christ by faith, hungering and thirsting after righteousness and expecting to be filled—nor do they know what it is to obtain the witness which Abel did, that they are righteous, nor the testimony that Enoch had, that he pleased God. "It is the Spirit which beareth witness because the Spirit is truth," and when we obtain the witness of the Spirit that we are righteous, by having Christ baptize us with the Holy Ghost, then we know in our own blessed experience, what it is which makes the gospel "the power of

God unto salvation (from sin) to every one that believeth;" and are prepared with Paul to say, "I am not ashamed of the gospel of Christ."

Let that soul who fastens his hope of redemption from sin, on the doctrine of Universal Salvation-remember that Christ has said, "if ye believe not that I am he, *ye shall die in your sins.*" This dying in sin will be found fearful indeed. It will be the portion of all such as will not "receive the truth in the love of it that they might be saved" from sin.

2. There is reason to fear, that very many who regard them selves as in a state of salvation, have mistaken the grand design of the gospel. They seem to suppose, that the great design of the gospel is, to save men from hell, at the close of their existence on earth, and that by looking to Christ to save them from the final doom of the wicked, when they die, they are then to live in a great measure in sin, inasmuch as their salvation is secured. Many, who say that they groan being burdened, under a sense of their vast uncleannesses, have no hope of being cleansed from sin, until death comes to their deliverance, supposing that, somehow or other, a bout the close of life, they shall be so cleansed, as to be meet for heaven. This is true of many who believe that the future doom of the wicked is, to be punished with everlasting destruction, and of many who rest their hopes on the doctrine of Universal Salvation. Many of both classes are supposing, that, a little before death, or in the very instant of death or immediately after death, something or other will transpire, that will complete in their souls the necessary work of purification, and make them fit for heaven. 'Tis strange that such vast multitudes should have imbibed such a notion as this, and should be resting such amazing interests and expectations upon it, when the bible nowhere intimates that any such change is to take place in any soul at or about the time of departure from the world. On the contrary, the bible does teach most plainly, that Christ is the only Savior from sin,

and that he came to *save us while we live*, and to preserve us blameless until we die. With this truth in view, we hear Zacharias, "filled with the Holy Ghost," prophesying and saying, "Blessed be the Lord God of Israel, for he hath visited and redeemed his people, and hath raised up an horn of salvation for us, in the house of his servant David, as he spake by the mouth of his holy prophets which have been since the world began; that we should be saved from our enemies and from the hand of all that hate us; to perform the mercy promised to our fathers, and to remember his holy covenant; the oath which he sware to our Father Abraham, that be would grant unto us, that we, being delivered out of the hand of our enemies, might serve him without fear in *holiness and righteousness, before him*, all the days of our life." Here is Christ our horn of salvation, even Jesus saving his people from their sins but instead of saving them at death, it is "*all the days of their life.*" Saving them too, out of the hand of all the enemies of their souls, unto *holiness and righteousness* all the days of their life.

With the same blessed truth in view, we hear Paul saying to the Corinthians, "I thank my God always on your behalf, for the grace of God which is given you by Jesus Christ, that in everything ye are enriched by him in all utterance and in all knowledge, even as the testimony of Christ was confirmed in you: so that ye come behind in no gift, waiting for the coming of our Lord Jesus Christ, who shall also confirm you unto the end, blameless, in the day of our Lord Jesus Christ. God is faithful, by whom ye were called unto the fellowship of his Son Jesus Christ our Lord." Faithful to preserve blameless to the end. This same faithfulness of God in preserving his people blameless, after enriching them with the blessedness of full salvation from sin, Paul recognises again in writing to the Thessalonians. "The very God of peace sanctify you wholly, and your whole spirit, and soul, and body he preserved blameless unto the coming of our Lord Jesus Christ.—Faithful is he that calleth you who also will do it." He says also again, to the same church, "but the Lord is faithful who shall establish you and keep you from evil." Thus plainly does the bible present to us the doctrine of salvation from sin through Christ in this life, and during all this life, while it never speaks of death as the time of salvation. Its language is, "now is the accepted time, Behold now is the day of salvation." And the bible nowhere regards any thing as salvation but salvation from sin.

You must then, my hearers, have salvation from sin while you live, or die in your sins, and where Christ has gone, never go. Any hope but this is baseless—for Christ declares that at his coming, he will give every man according as his work shall be, and that the unjust shall be unjust still, and the filthy, filthy still while the righteous and the holy shall so remain. Rev. xxii. 12. 0 that every heart who hears me, might be brought by the Holy Ghost, to cry out, how shall this salvation from sin be obtained?

In reply to such an inquiry I answer—The blessed bible tells us, "that the divine power of God hath given unto us all things, that pertain to life and godliness, through the knowledge of him that hath called us to glory and virtue; whereby are given unto us exceeding great and precious promises, that by these we might become partakers of the divine nature, having escaped the corruption that is in the world through lust." These promises we are also told, are "all yea and Amen, in Christ, to the glory of God by us," so that if we seek by earnest prayer and faith in Christ, to have these promises fulfilled in us, their fulfilment is sure. These promises are such as the following. "Ask, and ye shall receive—seek, and ye shall find—knock and it shall be opened unto you. For every one that asketh, receiveth, and he that seeketh, findeth—and to him that knocketh it shall be opened. If a son ask bread of any of you that is a father, will he give him a stone? or if he ask a fish, will he for a fish give him a serpent, or if he ask an egg will he offer him a scorpion? If ye then, being evil, knew how to give good things unto your children; how much more shall your Father who is in heaven, give the *Holy Spirit* to them that ask him." I have already shown that the design of this gift or baptism of the Holy Spirit, which we receive through faith in Christ, is to save from sin. To "sprinkle with clean water, and cleanse us from all our filthiness and all our idols." This is the baptism of Christ, which cleanses from sin, or makes us dead to sin, and alive unto God through Jesus Christ our Lord. If you would have this "gift of the Holy Ghost," this "baptism of Christ," this salvation from sin, seek it, with earnest prayer, and faith in Christ, and you shall find in your own blessed experience, that "all things whatsoever you ask in prayer believing you do receive." "Blessed are they which do hunger and thirst after this righteousness, for they shall be filled," and filled as we are assured, in the covenant and oath of God, "*all the days of their life.*" Come I beseech you, by faith, to Christ, for this salvation, and you shall find, that "the gospel of Christ" is indeed "the power of God unto salvation, to every one that believeth." All this hearer you must receive, or Christ will say to you at last, "I know you not whence ye are, depart from me ye that work iniquity."

O, it is a dreadful opiate to the consciences of men, to teach them, that though they sin against God every day, in thought word and deed, they may yet be saved from sin, when they die, and be received to heaven. It lulls into carnal security. It operates as a standing excuse for all the iniquities which men may chance to commit. While on the contrary, our Savior's doctrine, that if we believe not in Him as our Savior from sin, we shall die in our sins, and where he has gone never go, tends most directly and powerfully to arouse from the fatal slumbers of worldliness and sinful pleasures, to cry mightily to God in Christ's name, for deliverance from all our spiritual foes—and for strength and grace "to serve God without fear in holiness and righteousness before him all the days of our life." God grant that this may be the earnest cry of every soul, and be continued by every one of you until you find your feet in that "highway of holiness over which the unclean shall not pass." He that thinks that he shall certainly be saved from sin at last, will be almost sure to be saying, "a little more sleep, a little more slumber, a little more folding of the hands to sleep." May the Lord save us out of this destructive snare of the devil, and bring us all to behold by faith, "the Lamb of God who taketh away the sins of the world." Then shall we "obtain the witness that we are righteous, God testifying," within us by his spirit "of his" own "gifts," and "then shall we not be ashamed when we have respect unto all his commandments."

3. We may see it to be a matter of unspeakable consequence, that we do not trifle with, nor resist the Holy Ghost. He trifles with the Holy Ghost, who thinks lightly of the pollutions which God charges upon him, and will not seek to be cleansed by the Spirit of God. He resists the Holy Ghost who will not yield to the motives of the gospel, and come to Christ for the Holy Spirit that he may have life. If any of you my hearers desire the salvation of God-let me say to you as did David to Solomon his son. "Thou Solomon my son, know thou the God of thy Fathers, and serve him with a perfect heart, and with a willing mind. If thou seek him he will be found of thee, but *if thou forsake Him, He will cast thee off forever.*" The influences of God's Spirit are the waters of salvation from sin. They can be had by being sought through faith in Christ. "Ho every one that thirsteth, come ye to the waters." "If any man thirst let him come unto me and drink." "The Spirit and the bride say, come. And let him that heareth say, come. And let him that is athirst come. And whosoever will, let him take the water of life freely." Amen.

We invite you to view the complete
selection of titles we publish at:

www.TEACHServices.com

Scan with your mobile
device to go directly
to our website.

Please write or email us your praises, reactions, or
thoughts about this or any other book we publish at:

TEACH Services, Inc.
P U B L I S H I N G
www.TEACHServices.com

P.O. Box 954
Ringgold, GA 30736

info@TEACHServices.com

TEACH Services, Inc., titles may be purchased in bulk for
educational, business, fund-raising, or sales promotional use.
For information, please e-mail:

BulkSales@TEACHServices.com

Finally, if you are interested in seeing
your own book in print, please contact us at

publishing@TEACHServices.com

We would be happy to review your manuscript for free.